CW00505696

# THE PAPERBACK FANATIC

Issue 41

Published March 2019

Issue 41

Published March 2019


Edited by Justin Marriott

Assistant Editor Jim O'Brien

Proof read by Tom Tesarek


Special thanks to all of this issue's contributors.

Jim O'Brien, James Doig, Rob Matthews and Richard Toogood


Correspondence welcome-

thepaperbackfanatic@sky.com

# FANATICAL CONTENTS

# HEADS UP!

I know I am not the only collector who picks up books based on their cover motifs. Gary Lovisi of **Paperback Parade** often showcases galleries of paperback covers with whips or people drinking. One of my motifs is decapitated heads!

Pictured on this double-spread are six examples. I have more which I'll run in future issues. I hope you'll join in and submit your own selections.

*Jivaro* is a 1956 translation of the journal of a French anthropologist. Samuel Peffer provided the cover painting.

*Conan Road of Kings* is the Sphere UK 1979 edition with a Les Edwards cover painting.

*Soma* by Charles Platt is a Grafton UK 1990 edition with a Bruno Elletor illustration. I like that the decision made by the design team was that a massive sword dripping in blood from a decapitated head is less offensive than the male genitals it is obscuring.

*Madame Tussaud's Chamber of Horrors* is a 1985 true-crime account of 50 of the criminals immortalised in wax-work.

*The Franchise Affair* was first published in 1948 but I show here the later paperback edition (I don't own this one) as it features Debbie Harry prior to her Blondie pop fame.

*Attila the Hun*, as shown with a Bantam 1964 edition is actually a well-written and historically accurate account of the famous scourge of the Roman Empire.

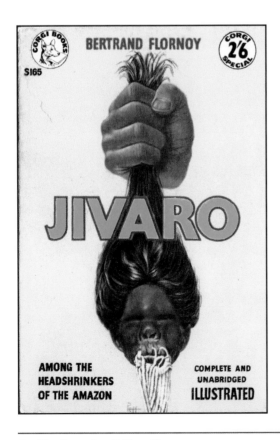

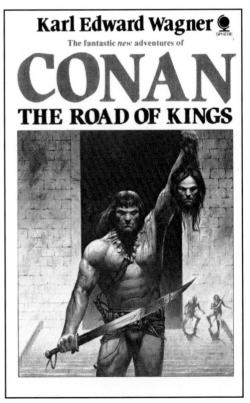

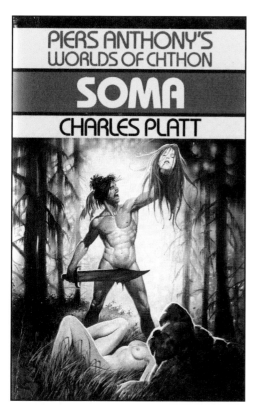

PIERS ANTHONY'S WORLDS OF CHTHON
SOMA
CHARLES PLATT

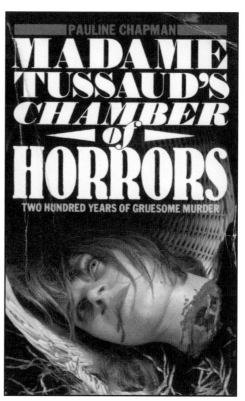

PAULINE CHAPMAN
MADAME TUSSAUD'S CHAMBER of HORRORS
TWO HUNDRED YEARS OF GRUESOME MURDER

Z3154 • $1.25 • A BERKLEY MEDALLION BOOK
Author of THE DAUGHTER OF TIME
JOSEPHINE TEY
THE FRANCHISE AFFAIR

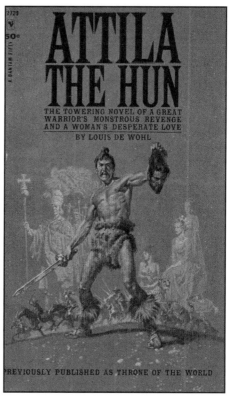

2720
50¢
A BANTAM FIFTY
ATTILA THE HUN
THE TOWERING NOVEL OF A GREAT WARRIOR'S MONSTROUS REVENGE AND A WOMAN'S DESPERATE LOVE
BY LOUIS DE WOHL
PREVIOUSLY PUBLISHED AS THRONE OF THE WORLD

# DOOM MONGERERS

Elsewhere in this issue, Jim O'Brien discusses the contribution of Brian Hayles to scripts on the BBC's early 70s eco-drama **Doomwatch**. These pages show the unofficial **Doomwatch** paperbacks, all of which were written by Kit Pedler and Gerry Davis, the co-creators of the programme, but they presumably were unable or unwilling to agree an official licencing deal with the BBC to put out tie-ins. Which is a shame, as the **Dr Who** books licenced at the same time were hugely successful, and at its peak **Doomwatch** drew in millions of viewers so had the potential to repeat that and perhaps extend the show's longevity.

In the UK, Pan published the three paperback editions in 1973, 1975 and 1976. *Mutant 59 The Plastic Eater* was based on the debut episode of the TV series, reusing on its cover the same photo that had been used on TV listings magazine **Radio Times** years earlier. Character names were changed and although the TV series was mentioned, it wasn't as an official tie-in. I don't know enough about the TV series, many of which have never been seen since their original run, to comment as to whether the other two titles were also unofficial tie-ins or unused script ideas.

The US Bantam of *Mutant 59* was published in 1973 and was followed by *Brain Rack* by Pocket Books in 1975 with a Charles Moll cover. *The Dynostar Menace* didn't receive a US paperback edition.

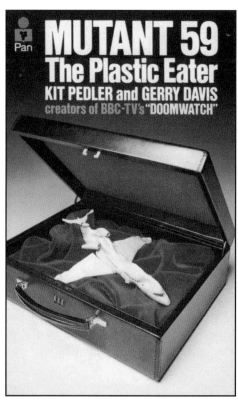

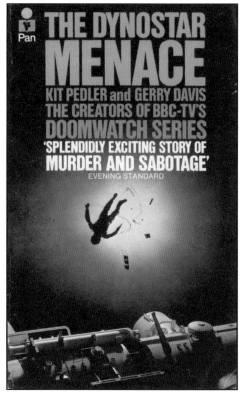

# E V CUNNINGHAM

The six Pans featured on these two pages were picked up in one expedition at Troutmark Books in Cardiff , irresistible at £2.50 each in very nice condition for their 50-odd years.

E V Cunningham was actually the prolific Howard Fast, who used this pseudonym on thirteen crime novels characterised by their titles all being a female Christian name, starting with *Sylvia* in 1960 and finishing with *Millie* in 1973. The books were unusual for their time for featuring heroines who came from normal backgrounds but who respond with pluck and vigour to their life being interrupted by crime or espionage.

Their tone varied, with the earliest being lighter with elements of farce, with the later books becoming more complex and dark. An example of the former was *Penelope* (1965), adapted to film with Natalie Wood in the lead role as a bored house-wife who eases the tedium of suburbia by robbing her husband's bank, and whose tangled love-life is her alibi as it involves the District Attorney and the Commissioner of Police.

*Helen* (1966) was a darker example, about the murder trial of an ex-prostitute and shoplifter who confesses to shooting dead a corrupt Judge. *Phyllis* (1962) was especially unusual as the lead was a female scientist, whilst Shirley (1964) was a street-wise kid from the Bronx.

New English Library reprinted a number of these titles in the late 1960s, all with photo-covers.

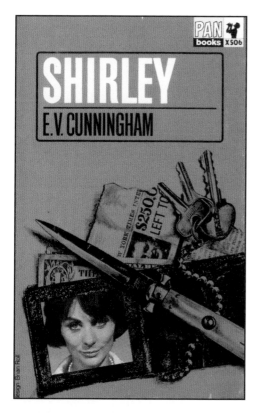

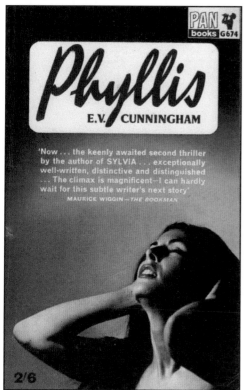

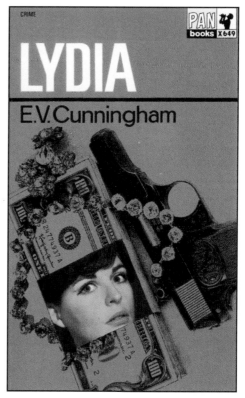

# THE HITT SQUAD

Over the next few pages I have reproduced 1972 correspondence between stalwarts of the UK pulp fiction industry. The letter is from Laurence James, who is now best remembered as the original James Axler of the **Deathlands** series, when he was an editor at New English Library (NEL) and looking to start a career as an author. It is addressed to Fred Nolan who would have been a commissioning editor at Corgi at the time, who continued the popular **Sudden** westerns in the 1960s when the original author died and would write several best-selling thrillers in the 1980s. Laurence was jointly pitching on behalf of Terry Harknett, another hungry young writer freelancing at NEL who that year would hit it big as George G Gilman with the **Edge** western series.

Laurence and Terry proposed 5 original series, and it got as far as contracts, a page from which I have reproduced below, which offered £750 advance per book. The contracts were with "The Atlantic Publishing Corporation" of whom I have no knowledge. The titles included-

Agents Anonymous: The Dutch Connection by Charles B Carver

Adam Hitt: The Bounty Hunter by William L James

NYPD; The Roundheels Murders by William H Adler

The Partners by James T Nolan

The books never appeared, possibly because it was a new publishing venture that was still-born, or that Terry's career took off with the afore-mentioned Edge westerns. Either way, I thought paperback fanatics might enjoy the insight to how pitches and plot summaries were written in the 1970s, and to imagine how the series might have turned out…

ADAM HITT - one.

Synopsis for:

ADAM HITT:

THE BOUNTY HUNTER

by -

William L. James.

Terry Harknett,
30 Stonebridge Way,
Faversham,
Kent.

Faversham 2909

84 Cappell Lane,
Stanstead Abbotts,
Herts.

7th September, 1972

Dear Fred,

Here are brief story outlines for the five series ideas we talked
about.  Terry and I realise that they are a bit sketchy but they
should be a good basis for our meeting on Wednesday.

To accompany them, here are a few random thoughts from me.  I imagine
that, if we are agreed on Wednesday, you'll want an outline of the
series concept for each one plus two more story synopses.

(1)  ADAM HITT   This story seems OK as a plot-line but it needs more
detail to establish the period which is, broadly, 1880 to 1910.  I'm
not too happy with his name either.  I suggest he might have a bullet
lodged in his skull which causes occasional unpredictable rages and
which he knows may kill him at any time.  It would be useful if he
could have been a friend of Grant, who died of throat cancer in 1885.
I've got a lot of ideas for plots for this series - snowbound in the
Yukon (where he meets Jack London): locked on an inter-coast train
carrying gold bullion (and a circus): a meeting with 'The Wild Bunch',
a visit to the 'Hole in the Wall' and a run-in with the Wright Brothers:
a story set on a Mississippi steamer (Mark Twain?) and a trip with
Theodore Roosevelt and his Rough Riders: the building of the Canadian
Pacific and Trade Union trouble: trapped in Salt Lake City: a
revivalist meeting where he meets Mary Baker Eddy: a run-in with Wister
who wrote 'The Virginian' in 1902: the Spanish-American War (maybe our
hero actually blew up 'The Maine'!!): a Klu Klux Klan novel
(1892 - 226 lynchings): plus cars, plus bicycles, plus Pinkertons etc...
All against the background of his job as a bounty-hunter at a time
when there weren't many bounties left.  Take your pick Fred!

Cont ... 2

(2) THE PARTNERS    This will be the A.T. and S.F. series.  Terry and I both appreciate your involvement in this one, so we've just done a single introductory synopsis without background detail - I quite like the plot of this one.

(3) THE CONTRACTORS    This will be a fairly formal Mafia-type crime series, heavy on violence, set in Europe, with the action spread through several countries.

(4) N.Y.P.D.    The 87th Precinct of the past.  I think we need two or three more major/minor characters in the cast here to spread interest through the series - as McBain does.  On this one I must stress we haven't done any research at this stage, as we obviously would do if the idea goes ahead.  I like this one.

(5) AGENTS ANONYMOUS    This is the war series that mixes 'The Dirty Dozen' with 'The Four Just Men'.  This synopsis needs one more main character introduced.  Basically, there will be about eight main characters, only about three or four of which appear in any one novel. They are all very rich, all with criminal backgrounds and each lives in a different European country and has a passionate hatred of the Axis Powers.  Again a violent series (like Sven Hassel) with the mise en scene enabling great mobility in time and place.  The characters can be involved in any aspect of the second war (or just before or just after) in any theatre of action.  I think this one could be a real winner(then again I am a bit prejudiced).

Just in case five new series aren't enough, here's one more idea to mull over.  How about creating a new Sherlock Holmes, set in the same period, but rather more of a traveller?

Terry and I both look forward to seeing you Wednesday to toss around a few hundred ideas.  Hope you like what you've got here and I hope there's the basis for something big for all of us.

All very best wishes,

*Lawrence*

1.  We open in a small town filled with angry
railroad workers who have come in from the point
where the line has reached.  They congregate in a
saloon to hear an appeal from three company
executives to return to work on promise of bonus
payment.  But the men want no part of this, being
interested only in payment for work already done.
The company men promise payment in full as soon as it
can be raised back east.  The meeting ends in a riot
with the executives narrowing escaping violence.
The proceedings are watched with interest by a man
named Julius Case, who then gets into the executives'
locked room to talk with them.

2.  A drifting gunslinger named Nick Striker rides
into town and tries to get a room at the hotel.  But
the coming of the railroad has inflated prices and
Striker can't pay the freight.  Case enters the
lobby after his meeting with the company executives
and there is a back-slapping reunion for Striker and
Case come from the same California town.  Case offers
Striker a job - guarding a bullion shipment.  Questions
from Striker will elicit only that the bullion will
provide both men with a solid future in the booming
business of railroading.

3.  The following morning a wagon with glass sides
rolls down the main street of the town, the sides
covered by canvas until it halts and Striker and

JAMES DOIG looks at some Australian paperback novelisations of films in the late 1970s and 80s.

# AUSTRALIAN FILM NOVELISATIONS

**While novelisations had been published in paperback format by Horwitz since the 1960s, these were mainly of US and British films and were published under arrangement with overseas publishers such as Penguin and Four Square. I'll focus mainly on Australian films and writers at a time when the Australian film industry was developing an international reputation with films like *Mad Max* (1979), *Picnic at Hanging Rock* (1975) and *The Chant of Jimmie Blacksmith* (1978) achieving critical and popular acclaim.**

Paperback imprints such as Circus, Sun, Unicorn and QB (an imprint of Horwitz) published cheap novelisations often written by stock writers such as Carl Ruhen and Keith Hetherington to cash in on the success of the film, and which often included black and white stills from the film.

Keith Hetherington (1929-) is best known as a prolific writer of westerns for Cleveland for whom he also wrote Larry Kent and Carl Dekker crime novels. In a letter (dated 11 May 1993) to Australian book collector and bibliographer, Graeme Flanagan, Hetherington spoke about the background to the novelisations he wrote in the 1970s.

"I know I'm outside your '50s and '60s era but the vast majority of my writing was done in the seventies and eighties. During the '60s output was fairly minimal while I worked as a journalistic editor for the Queensland Health Department (The Queensland Health Education Council, now defunct as such). My assistant editor was an American, Everett De Roche, in the late '60s, early '70s and he left to work for Crawfords [i.e. Crawford Productions] in Melbourne and was instrumental in my sending them sample scripts and storylines which eventually led me being taken on-staff... writing scripts for *Homicide*, *Division 4*, *Matlock Police*, *Solo One*, *The Box*.

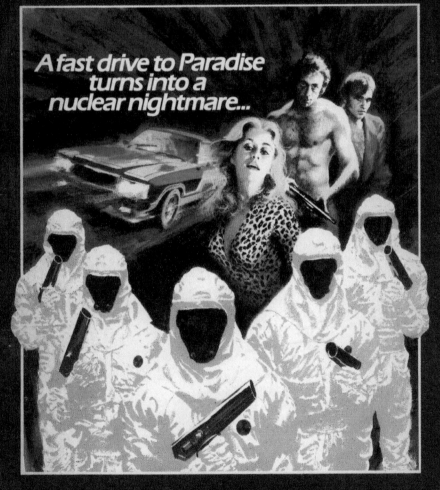

THE *CHAIN REACTION*

A fast drive to Paradise turns into a nuclear nightmare...

*by* **Keith Hetherington**

Also moonlighted a little and did scripts for Robert Bruning Productions, Sydney, in *The Spoiler*, a short-lived series ahead of its time. Also did some scripts for Roger Mirams Productions and Channel '0' (now '10') for the *Chopper Squad* series...During the '70s, too, I wrote some Books-of-the-Film, five in all: *Patrick* and *Snapshot* for Sun Books, c/- Macmillan Publishing Co. Melbourne, and *Harlequin*, *Touch and Go*, and *Chain Reaction* for Schwartz Publishing Co, Melbourne."

During the 1970s De Roche left Crawford Productions and went freelance, establishing himself as Australia's foremost writer of thriller feature films, one of which, *The Long Weekend* (1978) is a cult low-key horror film that is worth chasing up (it's available on youtube). *Patrick* (1978), *Snapshot* (1979) and *Harlequin*

(1980) were three of his Australian screenplays which Hetherington turned into novels. *Patrick* is interesting as a horror thriller about a coma patient with psychokinetic powers, while *Harlequin* is a modern day retelling of Rasputin's story. *Snapshot* is a psychological thriller starring Sigrid Thornton and Chantal Contouri about a young model terrorised by a stalker.

Hetherington also wrote the novelisations for *Touch and Go* (1980), a heist film with Wendy Hughes and Chantal Contouri, and *Chain Reaction* (1980), a road movie thriller about a nuclear scientist pursued by killers in outback Australia.

Carl Ruhen (1937-2013) was a prolific writer for Horwitz from the 1960s to the 1980s. Ruhen was an editor at Horwitz from

*Harlequin*
*Keith Hetherington*
*1980, Unicorn Australia*

*Snapshot*
*Keith Hetherington*
*1979, Sun Australia*

1968 to 1969. From 1969 to 1971, Ruhen edited *Man Magazine*. He also worked as a publisher for Ure Smith, from 1972 to 1973. His books fall into three distinct periods – youth exploitation novels in the 1960s, adult novels in the 1970s for Horwitz's adult imprints Scripts and Stag, and television and film novelisations in the 1980s. He also wrote series novels for Horwitz when required, for example Gothic romances under the name Caroline Farr (used mainly by Richard Wilkes-Hunter, see PF #34) and women-in-chains war novels under the name John Slater (used mainly by Roy Slattery, see **The Paperback Fanatic 24**).

Ruhen's first novelisation that I know of is *Crocodile* (1978), from a screenplay by Terry Bourke for a proposed killer crocodile film that was never made. In the 1980s Ruhen wrote five film novelisations for Horwitz mostly under its QB Books imprint: *Mad Max 2* (1981), *Duet for Four* (1982), *Summer Lovers* (1983), *Undercover* (1984) and *Melvin Son of Alvin* (1984), a sequel to the '70s sex romp, *Alvin Purple*. Horwitz also published the *Alvin Purple* novelisation (1974) and the sequel *Alvin Rides Again* (1974). While no author is credited to either book, the Horwitz archive attributes *Alvin Rides Again* to Carlene Hardy, the birth name of the prolific writer of Horwitz adult titles, Ricki Francis.

Ruhen also wrote novelisations of popular television soaps, including *Neighbours* (9 books between 1987-1989), *Sons and Daughters* (8 books between 1982-1988), and *The*

*Patrick*
*Keith Hetherington*
*1978, Sun Australia*

*Touch and Go*
*Keith Hetherington*
*1980, Circus Books Australia*

*Young Doctors* (2 books in 1988). These books were published by Star in the UK, reflecting the popularity of the shows there. Ruhen's last book was *Neighbours 9* and he died on 28 November 2013 after a long illness.

While Hetherington and Ruhen were responsible for most of the novelisations published at this time, there were a number of one-off publications, generally written by the original screenplay writer. John Pinkney is one of these whose novelisation of his original screenplay, *Thirst*, was published by Circus Books in 1979. *Thirst* is an original take on the vampire theme and stars Chantal Contouri as a direct descendant of Elizabeth Bathory, the original "Countess Dracula", who is kidnapped

*Thirst*
*John Pinkney*
*1979, Circus Books Australia*

*Newsfront*
*Robert Macklin*
*1978, Sun Books Australia*

and forced to join a cult. Born in England in 1934, Pinkney is best known for his series of non-fiction books on mysteries and the supernatural published by Five Mile Press.

The novelisation of the first *Mad Max* film was also published by Circus Books in 1979. The book is by "Terry Kaye", a pseudonym used by Terry Hayes, Brian Hannant and George Miller, who directed the film. A reprint published by QB Books in 1985 was published with the authors' own names on the title-page.

The novel of the acclaimed 1978 film, *Newsfront*, was published by Sun Books and written by Robert Macklin, one of the script writers of the film along with Bob Ellis, David Elfick and Phillipe Mora. The film is set in the years between 1948 and 1956 and shows the extreme methods taken by newsreel cameramen and production staff to get footage. The film won eight Australian Film Institute (AFI) awards, including best actor for Bill Hunter, and best screenplay.

A novelisation which received wide distribution through a respected publisher was *The Last Wave*, published by Angus & Robertson in 1977 and written by Petru Popescu, who was also one of the three script writers. The movie, directed by Peter Weir, is a celebrated mystery/supernatural tour de force with Richard Chamberlain and David Gulpilil that sees Sydney destroyed by a giant wave as forecast in aboriginal mythology.

Mad Max
Terry Kaye and a Frazetta cover
1980, Circus Books Australia

Mad Max 2
Carl Ruhen
1981, QB Australia

Novelisations of American films were also published by Australian publishers, for example Robert Bloch's novelisation of *Twilight Zone The Movie* was published by QB in 1983. A particularly scarce title is the Michael Avallone novelisation of *Friday the 13th*, also published by QB, which was published by Leisure in the US.

Other Australian films of the period were based on novels and were reprinted with stills from the movie to coincide with the theatrical release. These include Joan Lindsay's *Picnic at Hanging Rock* (1967), also directed by Peter Weir in a brilliant adaptation, and Peter Brennan's *Razorback* (1981), scripted by Everett De Roche and released in 1984.

JUSTIN MARRIOTT corresponded with Raymond Kursar in 2017, a prolific artist who specialised in romance covers, about his work on the 'Bronson' men's adventure series at the infamous Manor Books.

# RAYMOND KURSAR
## RECOLLECTIONS OF MANOR BOOKS

Dear Justin,
Yes, the PDF you sent of the paperback covers of the "Bronson Street Vigilante" are my illustrations. I would appreciate if you would send me a copy of the text before it goes to print, many thanks, here are a few too many pages of my Manor Books recollections.

**How did you enter the world of paperback illustration?**
I originally lived on the West Coast. After college, art school, and a couple of years in a local advertising department, I travelled to New York City with a variety of illustration samples in hand.

I answered a newspaper ad from an Art Employment Agency. I talked with the owner of the agency (a beautiful woman) and after showing her my portfolio she recommended that I return to the West Coast and produce illustration samples that I would like to do. She asked me to look at all paperback covers and pick the type of illustration I would enjoy creating, such as Western, Romance, Science Fiction, or Mystery. She said "when you have samples completed, bring them back and I will introduce you to an artist's representative and a couple of art directors."

I returned to the West Coast. For three months, I produced painting after painting with my directions set on three different art themes: Western, Romance, and Detective Mystery.

**Tell me about your paperback covers of the "Bronson Street Vigilante" series at Manor Books.**
I used a great male model for those illustrations. I remember him telling me "Ray, I have been working out at the gym for months preparing for an upcoming big box office move role, so I am pumped up and in great physical shape". And he was! I was lucky that he was available to model

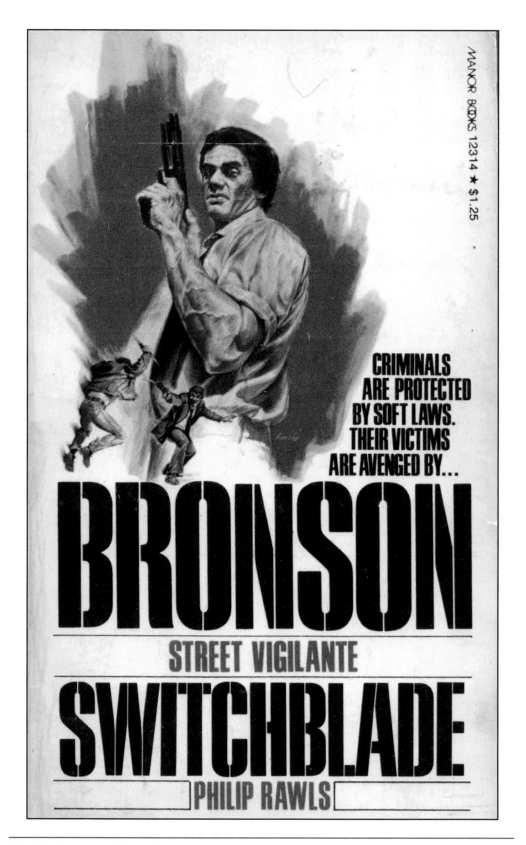

MANOR BOOKS 12314 ★ $1.25

CRIMINALS
ARE PROTECTED
BY SOFT LAWS.
THEIR VICTIMS
ARE AVENGED BY...

# BRONSON

## STREET VIGILANTE

# SWITCHBLADE

## PHILIP RAWLS

for those three paperback cover illustrations. Additionally, I photographed him for a couple of western paperback cover illustrations with an open shirt, rifle in hand, and muscular arm wrapped around a saloon gal!

Speaking about my first, here's a funny story about my first artist representative "Renaldo". He was a wonderful man and a godsend. I had finished my first soon-to-be-published painting for the paperback cover of a "Nancy Drew Novel". I remember walking into Renaldo's office to pick up another assignment and I noticed my "Nancy Drew" painting at the side of his desk and it looks totally different than what I had painted! I said, "What the hell did you do to my paining?" Renaldo blushed and said, "I just touched up the lips, the eyebrows, the hair, and her blouse and jewellery". I was pissed, but in reality, he had improved my art by 50%! After I calmed down and realized his enhancements to my romantic art had improved it, from then on all future illustrations I embellished my art using his suggested modifications. Thank you, Renaldo!

**Which publishers did you work for and any particular memories spring to mind?**
Those samples painted for my beginning art portfolio got me into publishing, paperbacks, novels, movies and Broadway Play art illustrations. Once published, those printed art pieces showed media directors what I could do and gave me entry into so many more illustrative

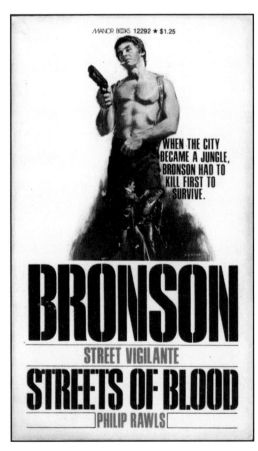

*Streets of Blood*
*Philip Rawls (Len Levinson)*
*1975, Manor Books US*

*Blind Rage*
*Philip Rawls (pseudonym)*
*1975, Manor Books US*

media assignments. I have worked for Ace Books, Avon Books, Bantam Books, Scholastic Books, Fawcett Books, National Lampoon Magazine, CBS, NBC, ABC, Good Housekeeping Magazine, and Broadway play posters for Serino Coyne & Nappi Producers, American Artist's Group.

**Any other memories of Manor?**
My memories regarding Manor books are really very good. I liked the art director because he knew what he wanted and gave me great art direction. I could not have asked for more than that! Manor Books always paid me my going rate and all my expenses, including model fees, costume rentals, photographic studio rental, and even paid for my 35mm film.

I recall after a few years of illustrating a number of romance book covers, their book authors called or wrote to the publisher requesting that they use me for their next book cover art rendering. My contracts with them were for first copy rights only, therefore, it gave me the opportunity to sell my second rights to South America and Europe.

In the past, some of the biggest magazine publishers have actually burned the artist's art or just tossed it out rather than store the art. Manor Books was different as they always returned the original art to me.

Unrelated, I remember creating an illustration for a poster for Harry Blackstone Jr., (the famous magician). I talked with him personally and he reflected about how he and his magician father (Harry Blackstone Sr.) had discarded & burnt hundreds of his father's old promotional posters from a warehouse. He regretted that decision, because 20 years later

*On this page and overleaf are three original pieces of Kursar art sold through Heritage Art Auctions.*

those posters were selling for $4,000 dollars each!

**What was your painting technique?**
Here is my painting process and technique: To obtain the illustration assignments, my representative or my many postcard mailers usually introduced me and that got me an interview with the art director or the editor. I then presented them with my art portfolio of com-

pleted and published work. If they selected me to create the art, they often handed to me a two-page outline of the novel, which we both read and discussed. Afterwards, we decided what art would best depict the story.

Then I create rough sketches or a small colour comp, which are usually 12x6 for their approval that week. Then I trundled off to look for photographic background material at the New York Strand Bookstore. After that, I book and hire models, rent costumes, and arranged for an hour photographic studio rental. At the studio, I would shoot about 5 – 6 rolls of 35mm film. After developing the film, I would review; print the best photos for reference for my finished sketch and the final painting.

I formerly illustrated in mixed media consisting of: Acrylics, Gouache and Watercolours on canvas. Now, it is all computer digital media of Acrylics, Gouache and Watercolours.

**Any particular memories spring to mind?**
I have been so fortunate to photograph so many male and female models over the last 40 years, many of which are now successful on TV, stage, and movies. I remember a tall, dark, handsome, thin guy who had purchased all of Basil Rathbone's designer men's suits (you know the British actor who portrayed Sherlock Homes in movies years ago). The paperback art called for a wealthy sophisticated powerful businessman and clothes don't make a man, but his Basil Rathbone's monogrammed suit sure made my illustration standout!

I also remember photographing a lovely female model named "Ava". When Ava entered the photographic studio, everyone rushed to peak over the balcony where I was photographing her. When Ava's eyes were staring at you, you would melt like butter. She inspired a great many of my romantic paperback cover illustrations..

I remember a photo-shoot day when I handed Ava a costume of a couple of two-inch wide strips of sheer fabric to cover her entire body. She was able to take that fabric and wearing only that, wrapped it around to inspire me to create a sexy, modest, WOW work of art. '

**How do you look back on your paperback illustration?**
I am a happy New York Illustrator! And now looking back on my early paperback illustrative work…what can I say it was the opportunity to be a New York illustrator, is something I really wanted! And those early paperback illustrations opened so many other doors in the future for the other types of illustration media, and everything from movies to TV, collectibles, movie posters, Broadway play posters, record album covers, greeting cards, and all of that was due to the first illustrating of paperback novels.

JIM O'BRIEN on Brian Hayles an author and script-writer who had an unseen hand in many of the UK's most beloved pop culture characters of the 1970s.

# ALL HAIL THE KING!

Brian Hayles is probably best known for his contributions to late sixties/ early seventies period *Doctor Who*, spanning the William Hartnell, Patrick Troughton and Jon Pertwee incarnations of the time travelling Gallifreyan. Hayles wrote *The Celestial Toy Maker*, *The Smugglers*, *The Seeds of Death*, *The Ice Warriors*, *The Curse of Peladon* and *The Monster of Peladon* for the show between 1966 and 1974. Whilst taken as a whole Hayles' *Who* stories are not necessarily the show's strongest, the author's creation of the Martian Ice Warriors definitely puts him up in the Pantheon of significant scribes on the series.

Hayles also submitted a fair few scripts to the *Who* production office that were never made, including *The Lords of the Red Planet* and *The Queen of Time*, now released as audio dramas by Big Finish. Fan Ewen Campion-Clarke has produced some tantalising *faux* covers for the 'novelisations that might have been' for these scripts.

The novelisations of *Who* stories that Hayles *did* get to pen were two for the show's early 70s Target Books range –*The Curse of Peladon* in 1974 and *The Ice Warriors* in 1976. Both have great covers by Chris Achilleos.

His contributions to *Who* aside, Brian Hayles was a wide-ranging and versatile scriptwriter and novelist throughout the 1960s and 70s, producing scripts for all manner of TV shows, radio series and films. For BBC TV he worked on early football soap *United!* between 1965 and 1967 (alongside various other *Doctor Who* alumni, including Gerry Davis, John Lucarotti and Innes Lloyd), as well as on episodes of police series *Barlow at Large* and *Z Cars*. Hayles was also part of the writing team behind the final season of historical drama *The Regiment* in 1973. On radio he wrote for 'everyday story of farming folk' *The Archers*, penning a tie-in novel for the series, *Spring at Brookfield,* at Tandem in 1975.

Yet as his connection to *Doctor Who* would suggest, Hayles seems to have felt most at home in that twilit territory somewhere between horror, fantasy and sci fi, and certainly that's what the majority of his work between the late sixties and his death in 1979 encompassed.

In 1969 Hayles was involved with the BBC educational series *Slim John*, designed to promote the learning of English overseas. Unfolding across a succession of short TV episodes, the show follows a set of humanoid androids, managed by the unseen 'Control', as they

mount a stealthy invasion of Earth, starting with London. 'Slim John' (Simon Williams) is a rogue android who befriends two humans, Stevie and Richard. Hayles provided scripts for both the TV series and contributed to the accompanying books, which appeared in a variety of European languages as teaching aids to support the programme.

Also at the BBC, Hayles wrote scripts for sci-fi inflected series *Out of the Unknown,* created by producer Irene Shubik. Hayles wrote two episodes, *1+1=1.5* (1969) and *Deathday* (1970). *1+1=1.5* is set in a dystopian future Britain where birth control across the population is managed by a central computer (the involvement of machines in health care and the treatment of illness was a recurrent Hayles preoccupation), while *Deathday*, concerning a

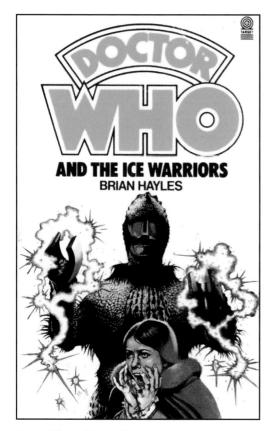

Doctor Who and the Ice Warriors
1976, Target Books UK
Art - Chris Achilleos

Doctor Who and the Curse of Peladon
1975, Target Books UK
Art - Chris Achilleos

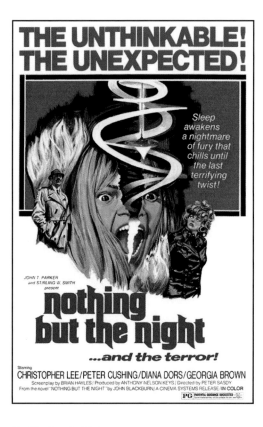

*Nothing but the Night*
*US film poster*

*Nothing but the Night*
*1971, Panther UK*
*Art - uncredited*

humiliated husband's attempt to murder his wife and pass off her death as the work of notorious serial murderer 'the kitchen killer', was Hayles' adaptation of the 1969 novel of the same name by prolific horror and crime author, Angus Hall … who expressed himself very underwhelmed by Hayles' effort.

For eco-horror series *Doom Watch* Hayles was also responsible for two episodes in the early 70s, *The Iron Doctor* in 1971 and *Hair Trigger* in 1972. In *The Iron Doctor* a sophisticated computer developed from an unstable wargames machine (this being the early 1970s, the 'sophisticated computer' is a vast, room-filling cabinet, all spooling tape, flashing lights and ticker tape printouts) begins to override doctors at the local hospital and to euthanize patients the computer considers beyond treatment. *Hair Trigger* deals with experiments in the use of computers to treat the criminally

insane at a remote psychiatric unit. 'Cured' patient Mr Beavis is – perhaps rather predictably – far from stable after treatment, despite his calm demeanour and smart new haircut. Beavis promptly escapes from the hospital and takes locals and doctors hostage at gunpoint.

In 1972 Hayles delivered his first film script, adapting John Blackburn's 1968 novel *Nothing but the Night* for a big screen outing starring Peter Cushing, Christopher Lee, Diana Dors and Keith Barron. Lee and Cushing are investigating the mysterious deaths of trustees of the Van Traylen fund, in a yarn that involves the transference of the spirits of the elderly into the bodies of children in a bid for immortality and the use of psychic powers to control others.

Extending his skills in horror writing, Hayles set to work in 1973 on a play for radio entitled *Lord Dracula*. The drama sought to tell the real story of Vlad Tepes, 'the Impaler' and his transformation into the Lord of the Undead. Peter Cushing saw the script and expressed keen interest in the project via his agent to the play's producer Anthony Cornish. When broadcast on Radio 4 as part of its Saturday Night Theatre strand in 1974 it was, however, *sans* Cushing. Instead, Vlad was played by Kenneth Haigh, with Nigel Stock as the unfortunate Father Benedek, a monk forced to bear witness to Vlad Drakul's transformation from noble Christian warlord into vampiric fiend.

Hammer's curiosity was piqued and they acquired the rights for a big screen adaptation of the play. Hammer boss Sir James Carreras had already been pressed by *Countess Dracula* producer Anthony Paal to consider a film about the real Count Dracula and Hayles' play was slated to be filmed as *Vlad the Impaler*. Somewhat ambitiously, Ken Russell was mooted as a possible director, with Mike Raven and both Richards Harris and Burton (as well as, of course, Christopher Lee) approached to play Vlad. Hammer though was on its last legs as a production company by this point and the project got no further than the discussion stage.

Between 1975 and 1976 Hayles wrote three horror-themed playscripts for young people, *The Curse of the Labyrinth, The Hour of the Werewolf* and *The Doomsday Buttons; a space fable*. These were all published in 1976 as part of Dobson Books' 'Theatre in Education' series.

*Curse of the Labyrinth*, with its riff on the myth of Theseus and the Minotaur, has a strong thematic link to Hayles' two Peladon stories for *Doctor Who*, both of which are also clearly indebted to the Greek legend. It was evidently a subject close to Brian Hayles' heart: back in 1965 he had already provided the scripts for TV series *Legend of Death*, a modern day reworking of the myth.

*The Hour of the Werewolf* (first performed by the Unicorn Theatre for Young People at the Arts Theatre London in 1975) features the Purwell family – archaeologist Professor father, son Paul and blind but psychic daughter, Diana. Set in the 1890s, the play features the Purwells visiting France so that the Professor can meet eminent Egyptologist, Professor Malatrice. On arrival they discover that Malatrice is dead, later learning that his vampish widow Madame Malatrice is the werewolf handmaiden of Egyptian deity Ophois the wolf god, to whom the Purwells are intended as ritual sacrifices. Although intended for kids, the play is a deliciously dark gothic chiller. There is even a touch of the erotic when Madame Malatrice, wearing close fitting widow's weeds but evidently <u>not</u> in mourning, sizes up Paul as a 'handsome young man…and clearly… sensitive.' Hayles wasn't yet finished with the Purwells, as we shall see shortly.

Also in 1975 Hayles wrote an episode entitled *Double Echo* for the BBC Playhouse supernatural anthology series *The Mind Beyond*, produced by old collaborator Irene Shubik. Revisiting elements of *Nothing but the Night* and *Hair Trigger* and no doubt riffing on Stephen King's *Carrie*, *Double Echo* concerns psychiatrist Dr Mallam's attempts to understand an autistic patient, the mute, 16 year-old Alison. Mallam discovers that Alison is a telepath and her mind becomes increasingly linked to the doctor's own. Soon, however, colleagues of Mallam's start to die in mysterious circumstances and the psychiatrist begins to fear for his own sanity and safety. Penguin put out a tie-in paperback for the series in 1976 and Hayles developed his script into a short story for inclusion in the volume.

A further creepy anthology series, *Supernatural*, aired on the BBC in 1977, produced by writer Robert Muller. Hayles didn't script any of the episodes but did adapt Muller's own story, *The Heirs*, or *The Workshop of Filthy Creation* for Fontana's tie-in paperback. Muller's yarn basically asks the question, how did Mary Shelley get the idea for *Frankenstein*.

Muller's answer? That before reaching the Villa Diodati, the young author holidayed at a remote Swiss inn where the owners were in the habit of stitching together corpses from the local graveyard to be marionettes in a macabre folk play. The tale they enact is a fairy story about a hideous Creature brought to life by his creator before killing a princess. Muller's episode has Shelley's biographer and his family visiting the same inn some sixty years later and witnessing once again the innkeeper's grisly performance.

Returning to work intended for a younger audience, Hayles next wrote the spooky Sunday teatime drama *The Moon Stallion* for the BBC, broadcast during the winter of 1977-8. *The Moon Stallion* once again featured the

Purwell family, this time journeying to the Wiltshire Downs to investigate the myth of King Arthur for irascible local squire, Sir George Mortenhurze. Feeling very much like a BBC response to HTV and others' slew of slightly earlier children's 'folk horror' series such as *The Owl Service*, *Sky*, *Children of the Stones* and *Raven*, *The Moon Stallion* manages to pack standing stones, old gods, warlocks, Arthurian romance and psychic powers into its punchy six episodes. Hayles wrote a Mirror Books novelisation in 1978 and also allowed girls' comic *Tammy* to run an adaptation (nothing certain, but it's unlikely Hayles wrote the scripts himself) in late 1978/early 1979, with art by Mario Capaldi.

Returning to the big screen, during 1978 and 1979 Hayles wrote film scripts for two fantasy films directed by Kevin Connor – *War-*

*Supernatural*
*1977, Fontana Books UK*
*Cover - still from the TV series*

*Warlords of Atlantis*
*US film poster*
*Art - signed Joe Smith, probably Joseph Smith who also did film posters for Ben-Hur, Day of the Triffids, 7 Faces of Dr Lao and Lady Frankenstein..*

*lords of Atlantis* in 1978 and *The Arabian Adventure* in 1979. Paul Victor's novelisation of *Warlords* for Futura (1979) has a preface by Hayles, while the tie-in paperback for *Arabian Adventure* by Keith Miles is dedicated to Hayles, who had died suddenly during production.

Oddly, given Hayles's background in horror and sci-fi, his swansong novel was to see him return to his TV cops roots with *Goldhawk*, a Heathrow heist caper published posthumously by NEL in 1979. All slags 'n' shooters in the **Sweeney** mould, the book concerns gangster Jack Fenn and his plan to hit bullion deliveries coming in to Mike MacKay's import/export unit at Heathrow Airport, all the while dodging the efforts of determined copper Alex Tindall to catch him. With some punchy scenes and restrained use of cockney rhyming slang, *Goldhawk* is a solid thriller. The book's cover is by artist David McAllister; evidently he or the art director at NEL knew just who they wanted to be in the movie version of the book, as the cover art 'homages' – amongst others – Sean

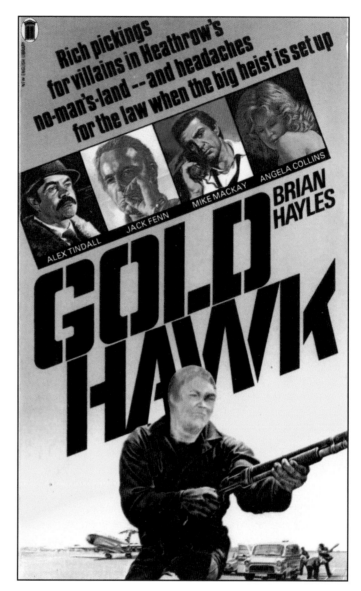

*Gold Hawk. NEL 1979. Art - David McAllister*

Connery, James Caan and Rod Taylor. You have to doubt, though, any of their abilities to cope very successfully with the 'west Lahndahn' accents...

Brian Hayles died tragically young, aged just 47. We can only wonder at what further scripts, short stories and novels we might have been treated to had he lived longer. Whilst never perhaps penning a cast iron 'hit', all Hayles' stories are solid and compelling narratives. Seemingly inexorably drawn to the dark side of the imagination, his work is quietly disturbing in an understated and contained way. A number of his fascinations – with psychic powers and extrasensory perception for instance, or with the role of computers and machines in monitoring or improving human health – still seem fascinating and relevant in 2018, nearly thirty years after his death.

JAMES DOIG looks at one of the more curious exploitation genres that enjoyed its heyday in the 1960s and 1970s in what has been loosely termed 'plantation pulp'.

# THE 'PLANTATION PULPS' OF NEW ENGLISH LIBRARY

**Virtually every major paperback publishing house issued novels in the genre, but the most opportunistic publisher was Britain's New English Library (NEL), which published about fifty slaver novels between 1968 and 1981. While many British paperback publishers got into the game, none were as prolific or varied as NEL's output of plantation pulps.**

Novels, songs and stories regarding slavery in the Southern US, and resistance to it, had long emanated from African-American communities, but these books, with their reliance on racist archetypes, were clearly not written for them. The genre mushroomed in the US in the second half of the 1960s. It was possibly prompted by or a response to the growth of the civil rights movement and the militancy of the Black Panthers and also emerged during a period of growing backlash against people of colour in the UK. In the midst of this, the genre provided white authors and readers with the opportunity to indulge in bigoted tropes and stereotypes. At the same time it potentially, and conversely, allowed the same audiences to express sympathy for captured Africans, and enjoy a sense of superiority vis-à-vis the southern institutions of the past and present.

One of the likely attractions for white readers was the forbidden titillation of inter-racial sex, given potent expression by the racist cliché of the well-endowed slave stud, invariably a captured African prince or king, who seduces or is seduced by the lonely plantation owner's wife. There is also a healthy dose of sadistic violence, particularly the cruel punishments meted out to wayward white women and female slaves who try to escape their lot.

In a survey based on 200 novels, Christopher Geist argued in the page of the **Southern Quarterly** in 1980 that the genre's appeal was predominately drawn from the way in which it pandered to long established myths and prejudices regarding the sexual availability of Black women and their supposed enjoyment of exploitation, and the sexual threat of Black men. Based

Robert H. Holder

**Manfee**

His giant body destroyed his master and enslaved their women.

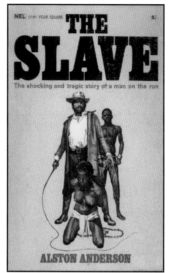

NEL 2181 FOUR SQUARE

**THE SLAVE**

The shocking and tragic story of a man on the run

**ALSTON ANDERSON**

**HOUSE OF BONDAGE**

THEIR SKIN WAS BLACK. THEIR EMOTIONS WERE WHITE HOT.

ALFRED BERCOVICI

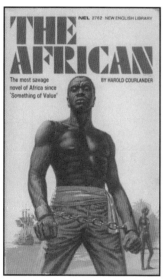

NEL 2762 NEW ENGLISH LIBRARY

**THE AFRICAN**

The most savage novel of Africa since 'Something of Value'

BY HAROLD COURLANDER

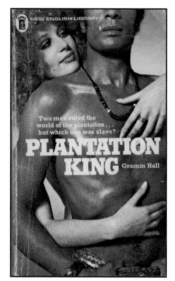

NEW ENGLISH LIBRARY

Two men ruled the world of the plantation... but which one was slave?

**PLANTATION KING** Gramm Hall

NEW ENGLISH LIBRARY

The story of a slave ship – and the terrifying truth of the 18th century slave trade
By Charlotte and Denis Plimmer

**THE DAMN'D MASTER**

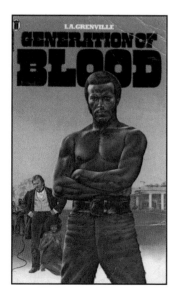

L.A. GRENVILLE

**GENERATION OF BLOOD**

NEW ENGLISH LIBRARY

**MISTRESS OF THE LASH**

By Robert Vaughan

2541 THE NEW ENGLISH LIBRARY

**SPARHAWK**

By Lionel Webb

In the brilliant, brutal tradition of MANDINGO and CHANE

on a 'complex mixture of folk beliefs about blacks and the psychological fantasies and insecurities of whites', he argued that the novels acted as a 'guilt-removing device' which offered 'the racially bigoted and frightened white reader an acceptable and controlled outlet for racial hatred and fear." Although the historical settings allowed readers a moral distance from the injustices of the present, the genre as a whole reveals much about the desires and preconceptions many white Britons, Australians and Americans held regarding Black bodies and culture.

The progenitor of these books was Kyle Onstott's *Mandingo* (1957), a huge bestseller which sold five million copies in the United States alone. According to Justin Marriott in an article in issue five of **The Sleazy Reader** in 2017, Onstott, who died in 1966, was an all-breed judge in American and Canadian dog shows and wrote books for canines. *Mandingo* was published by the family owned business that issued Onstott's dog books, the owner of which stumped up $25,000 for a marketing campaign, that included a free car give away at a national bookseller convention. The book went through three printings in just over a month, after which the rights were sold to Fawcett, which released it to great commercial success. A sequel of sorts, *Drum*, appeared in 1962, followed by several other Falcolnhurst novels co-written with Lance Horner. The prolific Harry Whittington, under the pseudonym Ashley Carter, continued the series into the 1980s.

*Mandingo* set the template for much of what was to follow. Set during the 1820s on a plantation in Alabama called Falconhurst, the novel traces the lives and relationships of Maxwell, the plantation owner, his son Hammond, Hammond's wife Ellen, and the Mandingo slave Ganymede, known as Mede. The novel includes a strong mix of miscegenation, jealousy, infanticide, murder by poisoning and violent death. The book ends particularly viciously with Hammond poisoning Ellen who has had Mede's child (itself killed by Ellen's mother), murdering Mede with a pitchfork, boiling his body in a giant kettle and pouring his remains onto Ellen's grave.

Ever an opportunistic publisher, and one which showed no qualms in meeting and stoking its audience's prejudices, NEL noted the success of the Falconhurst series and started its own line of plantation pulps in the late sixties. They began by repackaging mainstream historical fiction by people of colour as slaver novels, for example Jamaican-American author Alston Anderson's *The Slave* published by NEL in 1968, about a freed slave's journey across America during the civil war. In another example of a Black author's work being reissued with more salacious covers, Edgar Mittelholzer's Kaywana, trilogy set in British Guiana, was published by NEL as *Kaywana Stock* (1968), *Children of Kaywana* (1969) and *Kaywana Blood* (1972).

NEL also acquired the foreign reprint rights for the plantation pulps written by white Americans that US paperback houses such as Lancer and Paperback Library were publishing in the 1960s. One of these was Stuart Jason's Black Lord, Black Master series. Jason was one of the many pseudonyms used by the prolific American author of mostly crime and adventure fiction, Michael Avallone (1924-1999). The series comprised *Black Lord* (1971), *Black Prince* (1972), and *Black Emperor* (1972). They were little more than exploitation novels with not much to recommend them — the opening paragraph of *Black Lord* sets the tone for the rest of the series: *"His name was now Royal and he needed a wench. His body hungered and yearned and throbbed through all its mighty size and with every ounce of its tremendous strength for the warm, moist, tight inner recess of a wench."*

The series traces the fortunes of Royal, an African king and emperor, who has been captured and transported to America, and his efforts to return to his homeland. The success of the series prompted Avallone to write a couple of spin-off novels, including *Black Lover* (1972). Employing a common trope in the genre a plantation station owner's wife, frustrated with her husband's inability to satisfy her, goes on the run with a virile slave, a device returned to in the similarly themed *Kingblood* (1974).

Another prolific American author whose slaver novels were reprinted by NEL, in this case evidently without his knowledge, was Robert Tralins (1926-2009). Tralins published over 250 books, including *The Cozmozoids* (1966), *Android Armageddon* (1974), and *Pleasure Was My Business* (1963), a tell-all memoir of an infamous Miami madam that attracted a lawsuit from King Farouk of Eygpt.

Notwithstanding his pulp roots (he said that most of his books were written in sixty to ninety days), Tralins was a careful researcher. He grew up in rural Maryland where his parents ran a grocery store in a poor Black neighbourhood; his Black friends introduced him to their elderly relatives who showed them ankle and wrist chain marks on their arms and legs and flogging scars on their backs. His first NEL slaver novel, *Black Pirate* (1970), was a biographical novel based upon the life of Black Caesar, the notorious eighteenth-century African pirate. According to Tralins, he based his trilogy, *Black Brute*, *Runaway Slave* and *Slave's Revenge* (all of which appeared in 1969) on the authentic diaries and plantation journals of a slave owner who lived in South Carolina, which a rare book dealer had evidently let Tralins read but not copy.

Nevertheless, his editors demanded the usual mix of racy sex and violence and we get this in his novels in liberal doses. We have the standard plot involving a former Congo prince,

*Black Prince by Stuart Jason (Michael Avallone)*
*1974, New English Library UK*
*Art - uncredited*

*Black Lover by Stuart Jason (Michael Avallone)*
*1972, New English Library UK*
*Art - uncredited but Richard Clifton-Dey*

Brutus, sold into slavery where he works under the depredations of Black Gate Plantation owner, Jeremy Black. Naturally, Brutus is unable to contain his desire for Black's neglected wife, Deborah, but manages to escape the dreadful death Black had in store for him – to be eaten alive by pigs. Deborah isn't so lucky and Black cuts out her tongue and sells her to the first itinerant slave trader that passes by.

In *Runaway Slave*, Jeremy Black pursues Brutus with the intention of taking him back to the plantation (he is a $10,000 slave) and making his life a misery. Brutus is recaptured and in a particularly tasteless scene is forced to commit bestiality with a mule, but he manages to escape with a fortune in gold with the intention of making his way to Canada. NEL seems

to have thought the original titles too tame and they repackaged *Black Brute* and *Runaway Slave* as *Black Stud* and *Rampage* (both appearing in 1973). Later, when Alex Haley's *Roots* (1976) became a huge bestseller, NEL reprinted the Tralins trilogy in a single volume edition titled *Black Roots* in 1977. In an interview Tralins said that his agent sold the foreign rights of his slaver novels to NEL without his knowledge and pocketed the proceeds, the perennial hazard of the pulp paperback writer.

There were a number of other series, typically trilogies, which were first published in the United States and later acquired by NEL. Leslie Gladson's Captain Jacob King, Slaver Supreme trilogy, first published in the US by Lancer, comprises *King's Slaves* (NEL, 1971),

*Slave's Revenge by Robert Tralins*
*1973, New English Library UK*
*Photo - uncredited*

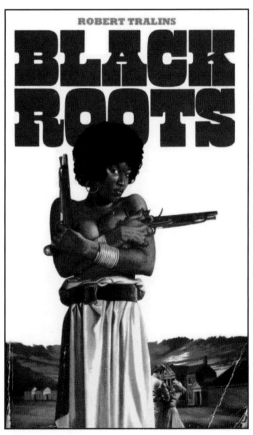

*Black Roots by Robert Tralins*
*1977, New English Library UK*
*Art - Tony Masero*

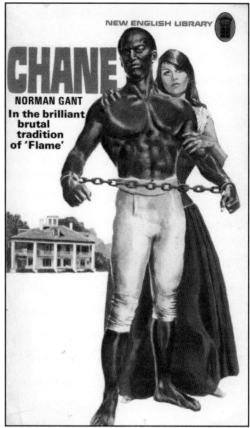

*Slaver by Leslie Gladson*
*1971, New English Library UK*
*Art - uncredited but Richard Clifton-Dey*

*Chane by Norman Gant*
*1975, New English Library UK*
*Art - uncredited*

---

*Slaver* (1971), and *Beast* (1972). Another Gladson slaver novel, *The Abolitionist*, was also published by NEL in 1972.

George Wolk, under his Norman Gant pseudonym, wrote a series of novels for Lancer about Chane, THE MAGNIFICENT NEGRO SLAVE WHO BECAME THE MIGHTIEST FIGHTER AND HIGHEST-PRICED STUD OF THE LOUISIANA TERRITORY. Although he is killed at the end of the first book, his sons take up his mantle in the second, in which as boys they are initiated into voodoo rites in rebellion against European institutions and religion. The trilogy comprises *Chane* (1968), *Vengeance of Chane* (NEL, 1969) and *Slave Empire* (Lancer, 1969), though the latter was apparently not picked up by NEL. All three were published in one volume

by Lancer in 1969 as *The Wrath of Chane*. The books are notable for their complex plotting and authentic detail.

Norman Daniels wrote a couple of plantation pulps for Paperback Library, later reprinted by NEL. Daniels was the pseudonym of Norman Danberg, who wrote for pulp magazines like *Phantom Detective*, *The Black Bat* and *Crimson Mask*, and also wrote some Doc Savage stories under the house name Kenneth Robeson. His paperback originals include Dr Kildare television tie-ins and crime and adventure books, including an international spy series about John Keith, 'the Man from A.P.E', one of which, *Operation T* (Pyramid, 1967), was set in Australia: A THRILL-A-MINUTE SPY

---

ADVENTURE AMONG THE SAVAGE STONE AGE TRIBES OF THE AUSTRALIAN OUTBACK.

Daniel's slaver novels include *Jubal* (1973), *Slave Rebellion* (1973) and *Voodoo Slave* (1973). In *Slave Rebellion*, the main character, Toby, was freed at birth because his slave father had died to save the plantation, Briarfield. However he is still considered a slave by Shawn Thibault, the master's son. Toby's lover, Julie, is kidnapped by Thibault, who takes her as his mistress and keeps her locked up in an attic at Briarfield. Outraged, Toby wants to join the other slaves in rebellion, but a lingering loyalty holds him back. When Julie is killed trying to escape, Toby makes up his mind to destroy Briarfield, but is torn when finds he must murder his master, the man who had given him his freedom.

Other NEL reprints from US paperback originals include Kenneth Roberts' *Flame* (1970) and *Blaze* (1972), Robert J. Hensler's *Mantee* (1971), Joseph Chadwick's *Sabrina* (1971) and Jeffrey Lord's *Jeb* (1973), all originally published by Paperback Library. Some of these turned the usual formula on its head and were about female slaves who use their beauty and feminine wiles to escape captivity. *Flame* appears to have been particularly popular as it was reprinted by NEL several times in the 1970s, and later slaver novel reprints, for example, the Chane books, were advertised as IN THE BRUTAL TRADITION OF FLAME.

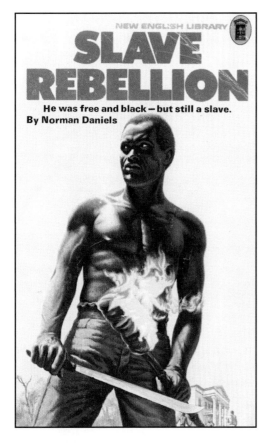

*Slave Rebellion by Norman Daniels*
*1973, New English Library UK*
*Art - uncredited but Richard Clifton-Dey*

*Flame by Kenneth Roberts*
*1970, New English Library UK*
*Art - uncredited but Richard Clifton-Dey*

*Black Lover by Clint Rockman (Ken Bulmer)*
*1972, New English Library UK*
*Art - uncredited but Richard Clifton-Dey*

*Black Lover by Clint Rockman (Ken Bulmer)*
*1972, New English Library UK*
*Art - Richard Clifton-Dey*

As the demand for plantation pulps outstripped NEL's supply of US originals, NEL's editors turned to their own stable of house writers for material. One of these was celebrated science fiction writer, Kenneth Bulmer, who was told by NEL editor, Laurence James at a London book fair in 1971 that slaver novels were "big." Bulmer subsequently produced eight novels under the unlikely pseudonym Clint Rockman: *Black Slaver* (1972), *Black Queen* (1972), *Black Gold* (NEL, 1972), *Black Ivory* (1972), *Sable Diana* (1973), *Sable Adventure* (1974), *Sable Mistress* (1974) and *Sable Ivory* (1979). Bulmer's novels are a cut above the standard slaver novel, though he includes the usual liberal dose of sex and violence. *Black Slaver* is set mostly on the high seas and traces

the adventures of Gloucestershire teenager, Richard Luckhurst, who runs away to Bristol with the intention of going to sea on the first available ship. After helping a huge Black man named Rafee in a fight, he joins the slaver ship Revenge, captained by a beautiful redhead, Emmalena Canyng.

*Black Queen* is set on a Caribbean plantation and opens with the brutal plantation owner, Jamie Moray, whipping one of his female slaves, Vuva, who is the daughter of the Queen of the Zinka tribe. Moray and his wife Frances use mainly female slaves as they are cheaper than the stronger males and they frequently work them to death or use them for their own sexual and sadistic gratification: The sight of the beautiful black body being tortured

*Black Summer by Roger Blake (James Moffatt)*
*1979, New English Library UK*
*Art - David McAllister*

*Black Reaper by Roger Blake (James Moffatt)*
*1978, New English Library UK*
*Art - uncredited, based on a still from Roots.*

aroused maddening lusts in Mrs. Moray. The slaves are captured by Spanish invaders, who in turn are attacked by French pirates, at which point the slaves overpower the pirates and become pirates themselves, with the goal of returning to Africa.

NEL's most prolific house writer was Canadian-born James Moffatt, who wrote numerous skinhead and other novels based on youth subcultures in the 1960s and 1970s under various pseudonyms, the best known of which is Richard Allen. He contributed to the NEL slaver series as Roger Blake and his books include *Black Harvest* (1977), *Black Reaper* (1978), *Black Fury* (1979), and *Black Summer* (1979). Although NEL's marketing emphasized

their fetishistic content, with sadistic and depraved plantation owners tormenting their female slaves, Moffat's books are invariably quite tame. *Black Fury* is set on the island of Montserrat in the Caribbean and deals with sugar plantation owner, the cruel Englishman, Sir David Noble, who is faced with dwindling profits and unruly slaves because of competition from Brazil and Cuba, soil exhaustion and the anti-slavery movement. In addition, Noble's feisty daughter is married to a gay man who wants to return to England, and his Black overseer, Joshua, has revolutionary plans. The situation quickly deteriorates when Noble attempts to rape Joshua's woman, Hannah, but she fights him off only to endure a whipping from a 'jumper' or travelling professional punisher. Joshua subsequently rouses the slaves to rebel and there follows the usual mix of sex of violence, including male rape, decapitation, and blood-drinking.

One of the last of NEL's slaver novelists was Leo Callan, who also wrote the NEL novelisation of John Sayles' cult horror film *Piranha* in 1978. Callan wrote three plantation pulps, *Black Sapphire* (1980), *Black Temptress* (1980) and *Black Rebel* (1981). *Black Sapphire* is representative of the books. Sapphire is a beautiful young woman, born a slave on the Kimber plantation. She attempts to escape with her partner, Benji, but they are captured and Benji is hanged, while Sapphire is sold to the highest bidder, the dissolute Courtney Blake. She turns to voodoo in her quest for revenge, but ultimately saves Blake from being shot and killed by his scheming wife and father-in-law and is given her freedom. There is nothing particularly original here and the series is notable only for the striking cover illustrations by Tony Masero, best known for his work on the long-running NEL Western series, **Edge**, by George G. Gilman.

Given the sheer quantity of books in this genre published in the US and the United Kingdom, the plantation pulp novel was one of the publishing sensations of the 1970s. Even in Australia, Horwitz's adult Stag imprint published some of the worst exploitation, including Peter Brand's *Rogue Black* (1977).

*Black Sapphire*
*1980, New English Library UK*
*Art - Tony Masero*

*Black Lover*
*1980, New English Library UK*
*Art - Tony Masero*

The unruly southern plantation milieu was a colourful background to play out the staples of exploitation fiction – forbidden sex and explicit violence by or against the establishment. Tensions run through many of the books as although the genre is often racist, sympathies are also evident with the freedom-fighting slaves rebelling against an oppressive regime. That said, the fact that the rebel slave leader often boasts royal blood suggests that égalité was not at the heart of these novels, even if liberté was a major theme.

African-American authors had continued to address their history during the 1960s and 1970s in a very different way to the house writers NEL and Stag employed to churn out formulaic novels of sex, violence and slavery. These wrested mainstream attention and ma-

jor sales away from the plantation pulps during the late 1970s. *Roots,* a fictionalised telling of Alex Haley's family history from the kidnapping of his ancestors in West Africa during the eighteenth century onwards, sold in its millions and spent months at the top of the **New York Times** bestseller list before becoming a hugely popular TV mini-series. Generational change, including growing opposition to prejudice in any form, rendered reading 'plantation pulps' an increasingly repugnant and outmoded past-time. Combined with new interest in Black genealogy, the market for historical stories from an African-American perspective swept away the 'slaver' genre, leaving it alongside blackface minstrelsy as a distasteful curio of white popular culture's recent past.

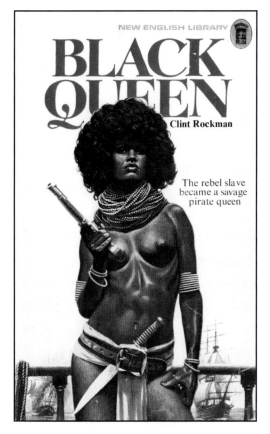

*Black Queen by Clint Rockman (Ken Bulmer)*
*1972, New English Library UK*
*Art - uncredited but Richard Clifton-Dey*

*Justus 3; Black Vengeance by Geoffrey Sadler (not a pseudonym)*
*1982, New English Library UK*
*Art - uncredited*

# "Slaving Over a Hot Novel"

"Slaving Over a Hot Novel" by Simon Redfern was a 3 page article on the phenomenon of the plantation pulps which ran in no lesser publication than **Penthouse** in its February 1973 issue. That the books were selling in sufficient quantities to draw the attention of an adult magazine is interesting to me.

Books across the genre are discussed, with a particular focus on the NEL variety such as *Black Slaver* by Clint Rockman, *Flame* by Kenneth Roberts and *Fury* by Mark Swanson. The tone is very much of disbelief throughout the article, and wry observations as to the sexual stereotypes paraded by the books. As you might expect, the article focuses on the sexual content of the books, quoting lengthy passages from *Flame* in particular, although one quote from *Slave Ship* by Eric Corder (Pan Books) are in a totally different league of bad taste.

Perhaps of greatest interest are the small snippets which refer to the production of the NEL paperbacks. Firstly, that the photos often used on the covers had been bought in bulk. I would link that information with the credit of "Lagarde" which regularly appeared on the back cover of NEL paperbacks.

And of the quotes from a writer of such books, who although never named, I'm confident is Ken Bulmer. "One of the more successful writers …. is in fact an Englishman, living with his wife and family and 12-year old Morris Minor in the Home Counties. Over a conspicuously English tea (jam sponge on a cake stand), he explained how he'd got into the business.

"I'm a science-fiction writer, really. It never occurred to me to write this kind of book until my publisher suggested it to me. He gave me a couple of books on the same theme. They were rather strong, and I told him I couldn't write stuff like that. I'm a very moral man, you see. Still, I wanted to build a rather expensive extension on my house, so I doubtfully wrote a couple.

"I've done four under this pseudonym now. The first two have each sold 30,000 in paperback and are being reprinted, the others are also doing well.

"I like to think they are moral tales. I disagree with slavery, of course. I try to achieve a balance between black and white in my books. In one of them, two couples end up together, composed of a black man, a white woman and two half-caste partners. The implicit ideal is that there will be a world in the future with no distinctions, a world in which all of the races have blended together and everybody is a nice brown colour."

Redfern finishes the piece by juxtaposing Bulmer's clumsy attempt to justify producing trash (other anecdotes do reinforce Bulmer's claim of reluctance to write in this genre) by quoting an especially flagellation-tastic excerpt from one of his books.

A thank you to the anonymous contributor who sent me a copy of the article.

ROB MATTHEWS presents the second part of his expansive overview of the Italian digest series which reprinted many key thriller and espionage paperbacks.

# SEGRETISSIMO
## THE SECOND ASSIGNMENT

**September 1965 saw the first release of the only American series that can rival Jean Bruce in terms of the sheer number of books published – Nick Carter. Though Carter had been around in one literary form or another since 1886, largely as a detective, the character was re-imagined in 1964 by Lyle Kenyon Engel, in the wake of the James Bond phenomenon, as an elite 'Killmaster' agent for the US agency known as AXE (incidentally, an acronym that was never explained). Carter's exploits ran to an impressive 261 books up until 1990, and were chronicled by Manning Lee Stokes, Martin Cruz Smith, Dennis Lynds, David Hagberg, Jon Messmann and many others.**

The first book, and the first to be translated, was *Run, Spy, Run* by Michael Avallone and Valerie Moolman, appearing for Volume 96 as *Agente N3: Sterminio* in September 1965. Italian fans then had to wait nearly a year for another, August 1966 seeing the fifth book *Fräulein Spy* by Valerie Moolman appearing for Volume 141 as *Nick Carter: kaputt!* although after that the translations came thick and fast. The rest of that year saw *Nick Carter: furore a Saigon* as Volume 146 in September, followed by *Nick Carter: una pallottola per Fidel* as Volume 151 in October, and *Nick Carter: la tredicesima spia* as Volume 157 in December.

Richard Telfair - Io ti tradisco, tu mi tradisci, esse ci
tradiscono
(The Bloody Medallion - 1959)
Art - Carlo Jacono

Bill S. Ballinger - Agente Hawks: destinazione Bangkok
(The Spy in Bangkok - 1965)
Art - Carlo Jacono

Richard Jessup, though he wrote in many different genres, is perhaps best known today for his 1964 novel *The Cincinnati Kid*, its tale of card-sharks in the high stakes world of poker being immortalised the following year with Steve McQueen and Edward G Robinson facing off against each other. Under the pseudonym of Richard Telfair, Jessup created the character of Montgomery 'Monty' Nash – a Europe-based operative of the Department of Counter Intelligence, tasked with taking the fight to the enemy. Of the five novels that featured Monty Nash, just two – the first and the fifth – appeared as a **Segretissimo**, with the last one coming first: 1961's *Good Luck, Sucker* was translated as Volume 107 in December 1965 as *Fino all'ultima spia* while June 1967 saw the translation of 1959's *The Bloody Medallion* as Volume 186's long-winded *Io ti tradisco, tu mi tradisci, essi ci tradiscono*. Monty's debut opens with his partner getting killed in Scot-

land, and the two of them come under suspicion of having defected, while his last outing saw him trying to expose a traitor leaking information from European embassies.

American author Bill S Ballinger had a multi-faceted writing career spanning over forty years which included radio, TV and film work as well as thirty novels under his own name and various pseudonyms. His most highly regarded novels – *Portrait in Smoke* and *The Longest Second* –both effectively utilized his oft-used technique of fusing parallel first and third person narratives to convey differing perceptions of the same events. In the mid-sixties, as with so many other authors at the time, he turned his hand to espionage and quickly penned five novels starring CIA agent Joaquin Hawks, the progeny of a Native American father and a Spanish mother, the first of which *The Spy in the Jungle* appeared in May 1965, quickly followed by *The Chinese Mask* and *The*

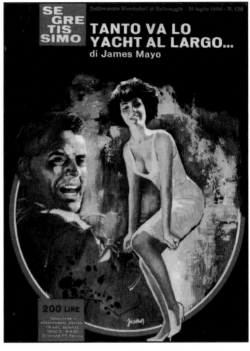

James Munro - Corriere di morte
(The Man Who Sold Death - 1964)
Art - Carlo Jacono

James Mayo - Tanto va lo yacht al largo...
(Hammerhead - 1964)
Art - Carlo Jacono

Spy in Bangkok. **Segretissimo** translated all three in 1966 for Volumes 114, 122 and 145 as Pelle di spia, Agente Hawks: rapido per Pechino and Agente Hawks: destinazione Bangkok respectively.

James Mitchell created the character of David Callan for television in 1967, originally for an episode of 'Armchair Theatre' but, after its success, then for his own series titled simply Callan, starring Edward Woodward in the title role. Callan was an assassin for British Intelligence, as was another character that Mitchell had created several years earlier – John Craig. Writing as James Munro, Mitchell debuted the character of John Craig, an assassin working in Dept K of MI6, in 1964's The Man Who Sold Death, where Craig's prior gun-smuggling escapades in Algeria bring him the unwanted attentions of the OAS (Organisation armée secrete). Craig starred in three more novels, the last being 1969's The Innocent Bystanders, which was filmed with the same title in 1972

with Stanley Baker in the lead role. The Man Who Sold Death was translated into **Segretissimo** Volume 115 in February 1966 as Corriere di morte, with the second and third books in the series appearing in 1968 as Volumes 224 and 244. The Innocent Bystanders was never translated.

One of the more colourful of James Bond's rivals in the 60s was Charles Hood by Stephen Coulter, writing under the pseudonym of James Mayo. Coulter was a friend of Ian Fleming, serving alongside him in Naval Intelligence during the Second World War, and later for Reuters and the Sunday Times, where it is purported that he aided Fleming with the gambling scene in Casino Royale. His own creation – Charles Hood – was, like Bond, an agent of British Intelligence, but he also worked for an organisation called 'The Circle', a group of Europe's richest businessmen who sometimes needed a man like Hood to keep the world a more peaceful, and thus more profitable,

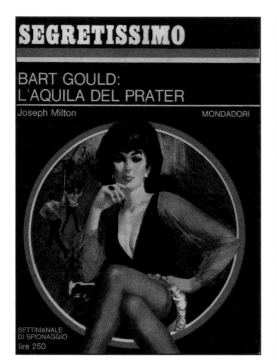

# SEGRETISSIMO

## BART GOULD: L'AQUILA DEL PRATER

Joseph Milton     MONDADORI

SETTIMANALE
DI SPIONAGGIO
lire 250

# SEGRETISSIMO

## OPERAZIONE "VARGO"

Robert Charles     MONDADORI

lire 250
SETTIMANALE
DI SPIONAGGIO

*Joseph Hilton - Bart Gould: l'Aquila del Prater*
*(Baron Sinister - 1965)*
*Art - Carlo Jacono*

*Robert Charles - Operazione "Vargo"*
*(Nothing to Lose - 1963)*
*Art - Carlo Jacono*

place. Hood appeared in six novels between 1964 and 1971, the first of which – *Hammerhead* – was filmed in 1968 with Vince Edwards in the lead role. *Hammerhead* and its 1965 sequel *Let Sleeping Girls Lie* both appeared in 1966 for **Segretissimo** Volumes 138 and 143 as *Tanto va lo yacht al largo* and *In due si spia meglio* in July and August respectively. The third and final translation was for 1966's *Shame Lady* which appeared as *Spia ... cevolmente ti uccido* for Volume 226 in March 1968.

Joseph Hilton Smyth created the Presidential agent Bart Gould in his 1963 novel *President's Agent*, but it wasn't Smyth's first brush with the world of espionage, for he had been convicted of being an 'unregistered agent' of the Japanese during World War II. Using loans of $125,000 from the Japanese government, he and two colleagues purchased three magazines and used them to print pro-Japanese stories and propaganda from 1940 until their arrest in 1942, and all three were

eventually sentenced to serve seven-year prison terms. The character of Bart Gould eventually appeared in eight novels over four years, but Smyth only wrote the first as Joseph Hilton, the rest appeared under the by-line Joseph Milton and were written by various house authors including Hal Calin and Don Rico. **Segretissimo** translated the first five, with *President's Agent* appearing in Volume 148 as *Bart Gould: l'uomo della Casa Bianca* in September 1966, with some confusion over the writing credits – the front cover credited Joseph Milton while inside the credit was to Joseph Hilton! The next four appeared in short order, correctly credited, as Volumes 153 (November), 159 (December), 166 (February 1967) and 174 (March).

Robert Charles Smith is a British author who has remained, over a fifty-year writing career, frustratingly under the radar when it comes to market recognition, due in the most part to his writing almost exclusively for the

*John Tiger - "Domino": partita a due*
*(Wipeout - 1967)*
*Art - Carlo Jacono*

*Nick Carter - Doccia scozzese per Nick Carter*
*(Spy Castle - 1966)*
*Art - Carlo Jacono*

hardback library market. Throughout the 60s, under the pseudonym of Robert Charles, Smith published nine novels for Robert Hale featuring Simon Larren, a killer for British Counter Intelligence. Larren, much like Matt Helm, was an assassin during the War who is pulled back into the world of espionage after several years of married civilian life. Only the first two novels in the series were translated, though not in the order in which they were first published. 1963's *Nothing to Lose* appeared as *Operazione 'Vargo'* in October 1967 for Volume 202, preceded by 1964's *Dark Vendetta* which appeared as *Cina: quota periscopio* in November 1966 for Volume 156. Several online sources indicate that Volume 175's *Operazione Apocalisse* is also a Simon Larren outing, but it appears to be a translation of another Robert Charles novel – *One Must Survive* from 1964, that is a downed airliner/survival type of novel. **Segretissimo** also published two entries of Charles's 'Counter-Terror' series of novels in

the late 70s and two entries of the 'Falcon SAS' series in 2001.

It wasn't just in Cinema where there was a proliferation of espionage in the early and mid-sixties due to the James Bond phenomenon – the TV industry also saw a glut of series developed to cater for the burgeoning popularity of the genre. Amongst the many series on both sides of the Atlantic, was one that gave a young Bill Cosby his first major role alongside Robert Culp – I Spy. Posing as a tennis player and coach, Kelly Robinson (Culp) and Alexander Scott (Cosby) were in fact the team of CIA agents known as Domino, considered the best of the Agency's duos working around the world. The series ran for three seasons and spawned seven original novels, all of them written by Walter Wager using the pseudonym of John Tiger. As well as working extensively in public relations and journalism, Wager was also an established writer of espionage, his first novel having been published in 1954. Sev-

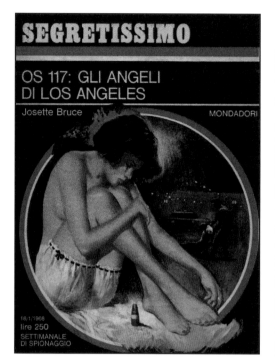

*Josette Bruce - OS 117: gli angeli di Los Angeles*
*(Les Anges de Los Angeles - 1966)*
*Art - Carlo Jacono*

*Gerard de Villiers - SAS: visita di scortesia*
*(Kill Henry Kissinger! - 1974)*
*Art - Carlo Jacono*

eral of his novels were filmed including "Telefon" starring Charles Bronson and "Viper Three" (filmed as "Twilight's Last Gleaming") while "58 Minutes" was used as the basis of "Die Hard II." All seven of his I-Spy novels were translated into Italian in the order in which they were published, the first of them "I-Spy" appearing as "Domino: operazione destino" in May 1967 as Volume 181. Subsequent volumes were 196, 205 and 211 from 1967, 217 and 256 from 1968, with the last novel "Death-Twist" appearing in March 1969 for Volume 275 as "Domino: Operazione Costa Verde."

January 1968 saw the first 'OSS 117' offering from Josette Bruce: *OS 117 – gli angeli di Los Angeles*, a translation of *Les Anges de Los Angeles* published in 1966, her first novel continuing the series her husband had created. This was followed in May with the release of the 75th and last translation of the original novels from Jean Bruce: *OS 117 – meglio spia che morto*, a translation of 1955's *Cache-cache*

*au Cachemire*. In total **Segretissimo** translated 75 titles by Jean Bruce between 1960 and 1968, 30 titles by Josette Bruce between 1968 and 1976, and 3 titles by François and Martine Bruce in 1990. This impressive total, though, has since been eclipsed by one other series which began late in 1968 – 'SAS' by Gérard de Villiers.

In 1964 de Villiers was a French journalist, working on a detective novel in his spare time, when an editor informed him of the death of Ian Fleming and suggested that he could 'take over'. The first 'SAS' novel came out a few months later and, such was their international success, de Villiers continued to write upwards of 4-5 novels a year right up until his death in 2013. The series introduced the character of Malko Linge, an Austrian Prince and freelance agent for the CIA, the term 'SAS' referring to his designation within the Agency and to the title, 'Son Altesse Sérénissime', the French translation of 'His Serene Highness'. Despite

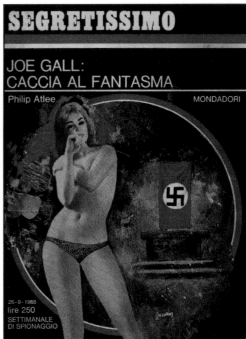

*George B. Mair - Operazione "Satan"*
*(Live, Love and Cry - 1965)*
*Art - Carlo Jacono*

*Philip Atlee - Joe Gall: caccia al fantasma*
*(The Irish Beauty Contract - 1966)*
*Art - Carlo Jacono*

working for the CIA, Malko prefers to live in Austria, restoring the ancestral castle and using the cover of international playboy to carry out the missions that take him all over the world. The first **Segretissimo** appearance for Malko was for Volume 253 in October 1968 – *SAS: Sua Altezza Serenissima* – a translation of *Rendez-vous à San Francisco*, the fifth book in the series first published in 1968. This was quickly followed by the sixth book – *Le Dossier Kennedy* – in November as *SAS: il gioco dei potenti* for Volume 259. 1969 would see five more translations, followed by four in both 1970 and 1971.

A curious side effect of the James Bond phenomenon was the obligatory use of an acronym for the villainous organisation that the hero has to endlessly defeat. One of the strangest to appear was SATAN, which stands for 'Society for the Activation of Terror, Anarchy and Nihilism' as introduced in the David Grant espionage novels of George B Mair. A

native of Scotland, and a surgeon by profession, Mair was a strong advocate for euthanasia and lectured widely on the subject. Besides his medical non-fiction, he produced ten novels between 1964 and 1973 with medically trained NATO agent David Grant battling various foes, including the aforementioned SATAN. The first offering from **Segretissimo** was the fifth book in the series – 1967's *The Girl from Peking* as *La ragazza di Pechino* in February 1968 for Volume 218. 1968 also saw *Live, Love and Cry* from 1965 as *Operazione 'Satan'* in December for Volume 262. Only two others saw print: *Kisses from Satan* in 1969, while *Paradise Spells Danger* came out in 1973.

One of the more hard-boiled of spies around in the 60s was Joe Gall, as created by Charles Atlee Phillips writing as Philip Atlee. Phillips, who was rumoured to have had CIA backing during a spell in the Far-East running an airline (his brother, David, was a CIA officer who rose to the rank of Chief of Western Hem-

**SEGRETISSIMO**

**JONAS WILDE:
L'ELIMINATORE**

Andrew York           MONDADORI

23-1-1969
lire 250
SETTIMANALE
DI SPIONAGGIO

*Andrew York - Jonas Wilde: l'eliminatore
(The Eliminator - 1966)
Art - Carlo Jacono*

**SEGRETISSIMO**

**PHIL SHERMAN:
MISSIONE 1**

Don Smith           MONDADORI

1-10-1970
lire 300
SETTIMANALE
DI SPIONAGGIO
Spediz. in abb. post. T.E.R.

*Don Smith - Phil Sherman: missione 1
(Secret Mission: Peking - 1968)
Art - Carlo Jacono*

isphere Operations), created the character of Joe Gall back in 1951 in the standalone novel *Pagoda*, but the series proper commenced in 1963 with *The Green Wound*. At this point in time Gall has retired in disgust from the CIA and is living in the Ozarks, when he is persuaded to come out of retirement to track down the mysterious Uncle Tom Asmodeus. Only two books in the series were translated in the 60s: *The Irish Beauty Contract* from 1966 as *Joe Gall: caccia al fantasma* in September 1968 for Volume 252 and *The Rockabye Contract* from 1968 as *Joe Gall: strage per gli innocenti* in February 1969 for Volume 274. The later *The White Wolverine Contract* was translated in 1978, and one of David's novels – *The Carlos Contract: a novel of International Terrorism* – also appeared in 1980.

Christopher Nicole was born, to Scottish parents, in British Guiana (now Guyana) and lived in the West Indies for 27 years before

relocating to Guernsey, where he still lives. His first book was non-fiction – about West Indies' cricket – but since then he has been astonishingly prolific, turning out over 200 books under many different pseudonyms. Most of his fiction has been historical but, writing as Andrew York, he also produced nine books chronicling the adventures of Jonas Wilde – the Eliminator. Working as part of the 'British Elimination Squad', Wilde made his 1966 appearance in *The Eliminator*, filmed the following year as *Danger Route* with Richard Johnson and Carol Lynley. *The Eliminator* saw Wilde growing disenchanted with the life of an assassin and ready to quit, but before he can do so he is given a seemingly simple mission, which turns out to be anything but. It was translated in January 1969 as *Jonas Wilde: l'eliminatore* for Volume 269, followed quickly in July by *L'uomo che morì due volte*, a translation of that year's *The Deviator* for Volume 296. Four more books in the series appeared between 1971 and 1978 (Volumes 414, 617, 678 and 760.)

The US publisher Fawcett, with their Gold Medal and Crest imprints, had several ongoing espionage series in the 1960s – the genre being eminently suitable for just such an occurrence, and it was profitable too – and several have already been mentioned; the Sam Durrell, Matt Helm and Joe Gall books especially were frequently translated. There were other series, though, and the occasional one-off that also appeared as part of the **Segretissimo** series. *Danger for Breakfast* by John McPartland and *Flight by Night* by Day Keene both appeared in 1965; *Torn Curtain* by Richard Wormser in 1966 (a novelization of the Alfred Hitchcock film); two books in the 'Evan Tanner' series by Lawrence Block – *The Canceled Czech* and *Tanner's Twelve Swingers* in 1969 and 1970 respectively; two books in the 'Manny deWitt' series by Peter Rabe – *Code Name Gadget* and *The Spy Who Was Three Feet Tall*, both in 1969; *The Spy Catchers* by Neil MacNeil in 1969 and one book in the Chester Drum series by Stephen Marlowe – *Drum Beat: Marianne* in 1970.

The last major American espionage series of the 60s to start getting translated were the 'Secret Mission' books by Don Smith that began to appear from late 1970. Donald Taylor Smith, Canadian by birth, lived for a time in Shanghai before settling down in Paris. He had two books published in the 50s, but it was with the 1968 publication of *Secret Mission: Peking* that he gave life to the character of Phil Sherman. Unusually for the espionage genre, Sherman was in his late 40s when he was coerced into working for the CIA, using his legitimate office computer business as cover. It wasn't until book 14 of the 21 book series, that he became a full-time CIA agent. Gruppo Mondadori, for reasons unknown, instead of giving each book its own unique title, resorted to giving each of Sherman's missions a number. Hence *Secret Mission: Peking* became *Phil Sherman: Missione 1* in October 1970 for Volume 357, followed quickly by *Secret Mission: Istanbul* which became *Phil Sherman: Missione*

2 in November for Volume 363 – and so on. In all they translated all 21 of Sherman's missions, finishing with *The Bavarian Connection* which became – naturally – *Phil Sherman: Missione 21* in March 1978 for Volume 744.

By the end of 1970, **Segretissimo** had reached Volume 370 and would continue to be published weekly up until July 1981. As of December 2017 it had been reduced to a bimonthly publication schedule but had still managed to rack up an impressive 1,638 Volumes – but I'll mercifully stop at 1970.

*Opposite page - All Gold Medals reprinted under the Segretissimo series with Carlo Jacono art.*

*Edward S. Aarons - "Sayonara", Sam Durell (Assignment - Tokyo - 1971)*

*John McPartland - Da pechino: il terrore (Danger for Breakfast - 1956)*

*Peter Rabe - Lo spionaggio è uguale per tutti (Code Name Gadget - 1967)*

*Neil McNeil - Gli accalappiaspie (The Spy Catchers - 1966)*

SEGRETISSIMO

"SAYONARA", SAM DURELL

Edward S. Aarons          MONDADORI

12-8-1971
lire 300
SETTIMANALE
DI SPIONAGGIO
Spediz. in abb. post. T.E.R.

SE
GRE
TIS
SIMO
DA PECHINO:
IL TERRORE
di John McPartland

200 LIRE

IN ORIENTE SI MUORE

SEGRETISSIMO

GLI ACCALAPPIASPIE

Neil Mac Neil          MONDADORI

29-5-1969
lire 250
SETTIMANALE
DI SPIONAGGIO

SEGRETISSIMO

LO SPIONAGGIO
E' UGUALE PER TUTTI

Peter Rabe          MONDADORI

3-4-1969
lire 250
SETTIMANALE
DI SPIONAGGIO

RICHARD TOOGOOD wields his savage sword as he takes in half a century of paperbacks devoted to one of fiction's most enduring characters.

# CROM'S TOMES!
## 50 YEARS OF CONAN IN PAPERBACK

**Conan the Barbarian has been a semi-permanent fixture of the paperback publishing landscape for more than half a century. And the announcement in late 2018 that Perilous Worlds was soon to be issuing new fiction featuring Robert E Howard's redoubtable hero only added one fresh milestone to a remarkable publishing legacy; one that has served to cement Conan's reputation as one of the most enduring and recognisable characters in modern popular fiction.**

Like his contemporary, Superman, Conan was a product of Depression era America. And equally, as with the Man of Steel, he was a wish fulfilment figure of sorts for his creator; one born out of personal frustrations and in reaction to the grim socio-political and economic climate of the times. Conan is the ultimate libertine created in the era of Prohibition and temperance, an itinerant in the period of US isolationism, a warrior from the time of appeasement. But above all, like Superman, a colourful irrepressible archetype who captured the imagination of a public hungry for diversion in tough economic days.

But when Robert E Howard shot himself dead in the June of 1936, Conan's prospects seemed every bit as bleak as the political outlook. Particularly when Farnsworth Wright, the editor of *Weird Tales* in whose pages Howard's seventeen Conan stories had seen print, rejected calls for other hands to continue the barbarian's adventures. Wright argued, correctly, that Conan was a very personal expression of Howard's creative genius and that no one else could possibly do justice to him. Wright's ethical stand seemed set to steer Conan on the same path to obscurity and oblivion that was the fate of the majority of story paper heroes in the post pulp world. It was paperbacks that provided Conan with an alternative route to posterity instead. But

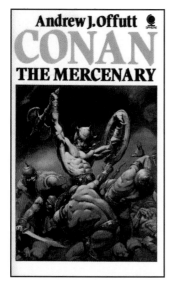

Andrew J. Offutt

**CONAN**
**THE MERCENARY**

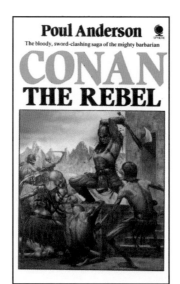

Poul Anderson

The bloody, sword-clashing saga of the mighty barbarian

**CONAN**
**THE REBEL**

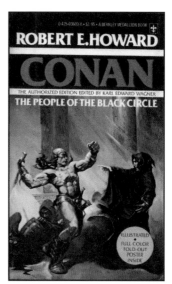

0-425-03609-X • $1.95 • A BERKLEY MEDALLION BOOK

**ROBERT E. HOWARD**

**CONAN**

THE AUTHORIZED EDITION EDITED BY KARL EDWARD WAGNER

**THE PEOPLE OF THE BLACK CIRCLE**

ILLUSTRATED
FULL-COLOR
FOLD-OUT
POSTER
INSIDE

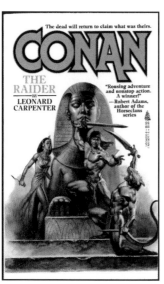

The dead will return to claim what was theirs.

**CONAN**

THE RAIDER
BY
LEONARD
CARPENTER

"Rousing adventure and nonstop action. A winner!"
—Robert Adams, author of the Horseclans series

FIRST MASS MARKET PUBLICATION

**CONAN**

John Maddox Roberts is a master of high adventure.
—Walter Jon Williams, author of Ambassador

AND THE TREASURE OF PYTHON

BY
JOHN
MADDOX
ROBERTS

TOR

FIRST PAPERBACK PUBLICATION!

John Maddox Roberts

**CONAN**

**THE CHAMPION**

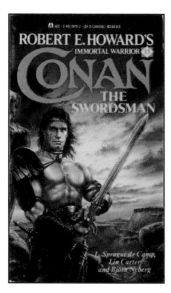

ROBERT E. HOWARD'S
IMMORTAL WARRIOR 13

**CONAN**

THE SWORDSMAN

L. Sprague de Camp,
Lin Carter
and Björn Nyberg

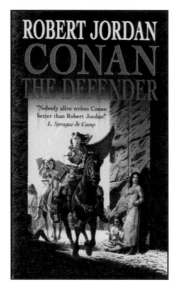

ROBERT JORDAN

**CONAN**
THE DEFENDER

"Nobody alive writes Conan better than Robert Jordan"
L. Sprague de Camp

SAGAS OF

**CONAN**

Three
Conan Novels
in One
Volume

L. Sprague de Camp,
Lin Carter, and
Björn Nyberg

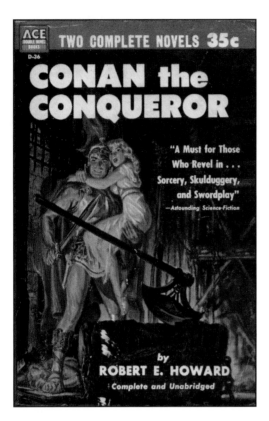

Conan the Conqueror: *Conan's only previous foray into the paperbacks field prior to the Lancer series was this Ace Double Novel edition in 1953. The book was packaged in concert with Leigh Brackett's* The Sword of Rhiannon. *Art - Norman Saunders*

*When masters meet. The iconic defining image of Howard's hero rendered by Frank Frazetta in 1966.*

it has not been a path without many painful proofs of Wright's contention.

The adventures of Conan were first collected into paperback in a famous set of eleven volumes published by Lancer Books between 1966 and 1971. This set, which was distinguished by the iconic cover paintings of Frank Frazetta, was to provide the bedrock of almost all Conan paperback publishing for the next twenty years.

Despite the passage of time, and the fact that it has long been superseded by superior editions, the Lancer series continues to provoke fierce controversy in some quarters. This is down to the fact that Howard's original texts were tampered with by the series editor Lyon Sprague de Camp (1907-2000). Worse still, a

number of unrelated Howard manuscripts were clumsily converted into Conan stories by De Camp who compounded his folly by then inserting Conan stories of his own into the books.

De Camp was able to justify these heavy handed interventions on the basis that he was merely filling in gaps in a saga which Howard had left unfinished by his untimely passing. The only problem with this argument is that there was no such thing as a Conan saga and never had been, at least insofar as Howard himself would have recognised it.

This enduring misconception that Howard's Conan stories are all episodes in some fragmented epic is all down to the well meaning enthusiasm of two fans of the charac-

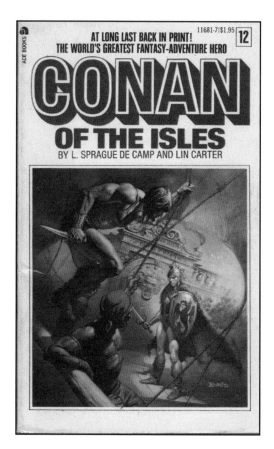

AT LONG LAST BACK IN PRINT!
THE WORLD'S GREATEST FANTASY-ADVENTURE HERO
11681-7/$1.95  12
ACE BOOKS
CONAN
OF THE ISLES
BY L. SPRAGUE DE CAMP AND LIN CARTER

*Aka Conan the Deplorable. Michael Moorcock expressed the feelings of many regarding the De Camp/Carter collaborations when he wrote: "Conan was never more dead than he is in these travesties of the original stories".*

L. Sprague de Camp
& Lin Carter
SPHERE
CONAN
OF AQUILONIA

*Frazetta's lost Conan painting. The original canvas was stolen from the offices of the bankrupt Lancer Books and has never been recovered.*

ter, Peter Schuyler Miller and John Clark. In the spring of 1936 Miller and Clark sent Howard their ideas relating to the ordering of the Conan stories which had been printed up till that point. Flattered by the two men's interest the hospitable Howard politely responded in a way which Miller and Clark misconstrued as an endorsement of their notion of a coherent and self-consistent saga. But Howard declined to mention to them that he had given up writing Conan stories by then, and was in the process of abandoning fantasy fiction altogether. He did however make the point to them that he had no idea what Conan's eventual fate would be, and couldn't even begin to predict it. So there never was going to be any conclusion to

Conan's adventures, no narrative culmination to be attained.

Nevertheless this cordial gesture on Howard's part encouraged Miller and Clark to compile their "A Probable Outline of Conan's Career" published in *The Hyborian Age* (1938) which De Camp was to adopt as the guiding principle for the Lancer series and use to legitimize his control over all subsequent Conan publishing.

De Camp wrote the majority of his own Conan stories in collaboration with Lin Carter (1930-1988). All too aware of his own shortcomings for the task he hoped an amalgam of their contrasting approaches would produce an acceptable mimicry of Howard's pneumatic style. He could hardly have been proven any more misguided. Despite the occasional flash of inventiveness De Camp and Carter's Conan stories are hopeless. The two full length novels which the pair contributed to the Lancer series are especially poor. *Conan of the Isles* indeed remains a low point in the history of Conan publishing, one which Michael Moorcock was moved to deride as "mindless, silly, heartless stuff which would disgrace even a schoolboy imitator".

De Camp's original vision was for the Conan saga to run to twelve volumes, encompassing every stage of Conan's career from reckless youth to grizzled old king. Much to his frustration Lancer Books went bust in 1973 before the twelfth and final title, *Conan of Aquilonia*, could be published. The collapse of the company tied up the entire series in complex litigation. The consequence of this being that Conan effectively vanished from the US paperback scene; ironically at the very moment when the success of Marvel Comics' various Conan magazines was stimulating an upsurge of interest in the original stories.

Conan did not return to US paperbacks until 1977 when Glenn Lord, the executor of Howard's estate, brokered a deal with Berkley Books to reprint the original **Weird Tales** texts of the Conan stories in a six volume set edited by fantasy writer and Howard buff Karl Edward Wagner (1945-1994). If *Conan of the Isles* marked a nadir in the character's fortunes then the Berkley series was nothing less than a triumphant celebration of Howard's work. Not only did it benefit from Wagner's scrupulous editorial diligence but it was graced too by striking covers courtesy of Frazetta protégé Ken Kelly. These covers were so impressive that Berkley included them as fold out posters inside the books.

The Berkley titles were the best Conan books published up till that point. They remain fondly remembered to this day and would probably never have been superseded had Berkley not pulled the plug on them with the series only half complete. But, horrified at the prospect of losing control of a property which

he saw as his own personal milch cow, De Camp rushed through a deal with Ace Books to flood the market with reprints of the original Lancer titles. By a strange quirk of happenstance Ace had been the very first publisher to issue a Conan paperback almost a quarter of a century earlier. Whatever their editorial flaws and failings these books proved very popular with some of the titles going through twenty printings. In the face of such determined competition Berkley terminated their own Conan series, although the company did persevere with its extended catalogue of other Howard works.

However much Conan himself might well have relished a publishing war it quickly became clear that a free-for-all of this nature was to no one's benefit. And so a company called Conan Properties Inc was formed to represent all the competing interests laying claim to the character. One of CPI's first actions was to broker a contract for six new Conan books. This contract was signed with Bantam Books, presumably so as not to be seen to favour any of the architects behind the previous deals.

The Bantam series is the very definition of a curate's egg. Three of the books represent decent stabs at the tricky discipline of pastiche writing, while the remainder comprise some of the worst Conan stories ever written.

It is a measure of De Camp's proprietary attitude towards Conan that he secured the writing assignment of no less than three of the Bantam books for himself. Suffice it to say that these three books are **not** the decent stabs at pastiche writing previously alluded to. *Conan the Swordsman* is a collection of short stories in the vein of the earlier Lancer volumes and roughly on a par with them in terms of quality. *Conan the Liberator*, written in collaboration with Carter, is a novel which tells the story of Conan's seizure of the kingship of Aquilonia. As difficult as it can be sometimes to remain objective when discussing De Camp and Carter's collaborations it is worth making the point that Carter himself dismissed **CONAN THE LIBERATOR** as "simply awful". The one significant facet to **CONAN AND THE SPIDER GOD** is that it remains the only Conan book published solely under De Camp's name. And it is an indefensibly wretched novel; so shoddily plotted and badly written that it beggars belief how a writer of De Camp's stature and reputation could so cheerfully have put his name to it. The suggestion has been made that De Camp actually delegated much of the writing of the book to his wife. There may indeed be some currency in this idea. For as misconceived as De Camp's previous treatments of Conan may have been they had never before descended to the level of churlish parody found in this book.

The three other titles in the Bantam set are all more palatable, having been written by established fantasy professionals and professed Howard fans into the bargain. Poul Anderson (1926-2001), who at the outset of his career had produced one of the finest novels of swords and sorcery ever written in THE BROKEN SWORD, contributed CONAN THE REBEL, a tale of Conan's time as a pirate chief in the company of the beguiling Bêlit, Howard's self styled Queen of the Black Coast. Karl Edward Wagner wrote CONAN: THE ROAD OF KINGS, while Andrew Offutt (1934-2013) offered up CONAN: THE SWORD OF SKELOS.

What is interesting about Offutt's novel is that it is a sequel to an earlier novella he had written called **CONAN AND THE SORCERER.** This had originally been published in 1978 in a trade paperback format by the Sundridge Press, sumptuously illustrated by Spanish artist Esteban Maroto. The book was republished in a mass market edition by Ace Books in 1979. Offutt's intention was to follow up the Ace issue with a direct sequel called *Conan the Mercenary* which would explain how Conan regained his soul having been deprived of it in the previous novella. This book would then lead directly into *Conan: The Sword of Skelos*. However because Wagner was so late in delivering his own manuscript Offutt's book found itself promoted in Bantam's publishing schedule thereby appearing more than eighteen months in advance of *Conan the Mercenary*. One imagines that this must have resulted in a degree of consternation for readers of the period perplexed enough already in trying to follow a story split between two different publishers without the added headache of having it published out of sequence. It was left to Sphere Books in the UK to eventually deliver upon Offutt's vision by combining the two novellas into one volume and immediately following it up with their own edition of *Conan: The Sword of Skelos*.

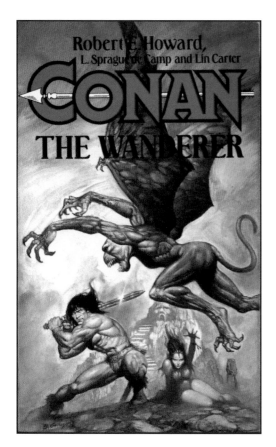

*The Blas Gallego designs were a last ditch effort by Sphere to arrest dwindling sales in the late 80s. The attempt failed but left behind an impressive, if largely unsung, addition to Conan's pictorial legacy.*

For all the editorial issues and textual problems they inherited from their Lancer sources the Sphere books still exert a nostalgic appeal for most UK Conan fans, and have much to recommend them besides. The Sphere edition of **CONAN OF AQUILONIA**, for example, is the only one to boast Frank Frazetta's commis-

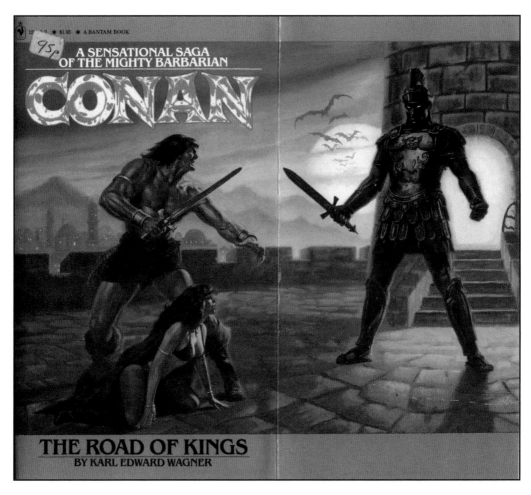

A SENSATIONAL SAGA
OF THE MIGHTY BARBARIAN
## CONAN
THE ROAD OF KINGS
BY KARL EDWARD WAGNER

*Bob Larkin's sensational gatefold cover for the Bantam edition of Wagner's novel. Larkin's work is notable for the great facial grimaces which invest his figures with life. Like Boris Vallejo before him, and Doug Beekman afterwards, Larkin came to Conan book covers after graduating from Marvel's Savage Sword of Conan magazine.*

sioned cover design. The original canvas had been stolen several years earlier, around the time of Lancer's collapse, but not before a transparency had been delivered to Sphere.

The cover art has always been a significant feature of Conan paperback publishing, and the Sphere set is no different. Although it slavishly regurgitated the original Lancer designs to begin with it did eventually diversify into original art commissioned, primarily, from Les Edwards. Some of Edwards' efforts, such as that found on *Conan the Liberator*, tried that little too hard to be different. The legacy of Frazetta was as all pervasive then as it remains today and one which all Conan artists struggle

to escape from. But some of Edwards' paintings, particularly those he contributed to *Conan the Rebel* and *Conan: The Raod of Kings*, still pack a punch. Towards the end of the series' life Sphere repackaged all the books in designs supplied by Blas Gallego.

Sphere's association with Conan began in 1973 and was to continue for the next eighteen years. In that time Sphere issued an impressive thirty four different titles, including two omnibus editions, which brought under the one umbrella books produced by most of the brawling barbarian's Stateside publishers: Lancer, Ace, Bantam and, eventually, Tor. By the time the series eventually ended Sphere itself was no more, the company having been bought up by Robert Maxwell's Pergamon Publishing Corporation. The final few issues appeared under the company's Orbit logo.

Back across the Atlantic Bantam declined to persevere with Conan after publishing De Camp and Carter's novelisation of the 1982 Arnold Schwarzenegger vehicle *Conan the Barbarian*. Sales were clearly the determining factor in this decision. But Bantam may have concluded that the fantasy revival of the mid 1970s had simply run its course. If this was the case then it was a hasty and premature judgement as the subsequent success of the film not only galvanised renewed interest in Conan par-

*Conan has enjoyed mixed fortunes at the movies. But a fourth film, with an ageing Schwarzenegger back in the part, has long been ~~threatened~~ promised.*

ticularly but in swords and sorcery stories in general.

But if Bantam was a victim of its own misjudgement then the fledgling imprint of Tor Books was the beneficiary of fortuitous timing. In a different climate it would never have been in a position to compete with the big paperback publishers for a property like Conan. Tor was then a long way from becoming the corporate behemoth it is today. But there was a general indifference towards fantasy prevailing amongst publishers and by the time the huge returns brought in by the film had persuaded them otherwise Conan was already safely ensconced in his new publishing home.

There is no other publisher in the whole history of Conan fiction which can boast a comparable scale of output or duration of association with the character than Tor. Not unless one counts Marvel Comics. Between 1982 and 1997 Tor published forty two original Conan novels, with one further title following belatedly in 2003. It also published reprints of the Bantam set.

Tor's resources were so small to begin with that it was not even in a position to distribute its own books. And this is reflected in the small pool of literary talent it could draw upon when it came to the writing of its Conan books. But it continued to ride the luck it had known in winning the property by having the first seven volumes in its Conan catalogue written for it by Robert Jordan.

Robert Jordan was the pen name of James Oliver Rigney Jr (1948–2007), a writer better known now because of his monumental **Wheel of Time** extravaganza than he ever was back then. Jordan was a far better writer than Lin Carter had ever been and had a better grasp of Conan's character than De Camp ever displayed. No one would ever claim that his Conan books boast the psychological depths or artistic merits of Howard's original stories, but they are bright and breezy reads which make a good use of the superficial aspects of the original works.

Jordan's Conan books are good fantasy novels, with imaginative flourishes, strong scenarios and solid characters. They are certainly better written than many of the pitiful attempts at pastiche Conan that had preceded them. If his novels are reflective of any particular influence then it is probably the thousands of pages of Conan comic strips written by Roy Thomas for Marvel Comics between 1970 and 1980. Jordan even went to the trouble of co-opting Thomas's character Red Sonja into the books albeit under the name of Karela the Red Hawk; an alias as flimsy as the gossamer garments on one of Conan's quailing girlfriends. It seems only fitting therefore that it should be Jordan who novelised the second Schwarzenegger film, *Conan the Destroyer*, for which Thomas had co-written the story.

A small coterie of five writers was responsible for the vast majority of the remaining books in the Tor series. For some of them, like Steve Perry, this was clearly just work for hire with the results being as uninspired as one would expect them to be. For others, such as John Maddox Roberts, there was clearly more of a genuine interest in the material.

Where all the books really suffered was with De Camp's insistence that the tone of them be kept palatable for a teenage readership, with the graphic violence and sexual content moderated accordingly. The irony was completely lost on him that it was precisely these elements that the average teenager would, in all likelihood, buy the books hoping to find.

There is no question that De Camp's fascination with Conan was a genuine interest but he was always conflicted by his own conviction that Howard was a stunted adolescent whose work was really fit only for juveniles, and he projected this attitude onto the Tor books thereby tailoring them to conform to his own prejudices.

The Tor books were never helped either by the tired and formulaic cover designs. Some of these were the work of Boris Vallejo, a ubiquitous figure in 1980s paperback illustration, but the vast majority of them were contributed by Ken Kelly. Kelly recycled the same stock composition of Conan, monster and cringing

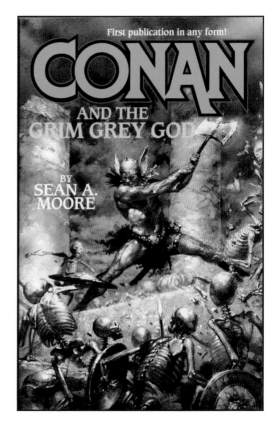

Conan and the Grim Grey God: *Conan of the Argonauts? Actually one of too few contributions to the Tor series made by artistic maestro Doug Beekman.*

heroine ad infinitum. It was all a far cry from the inspired imagery he had contributed to the truncated Berkley set of a decade earlier. But in some ways it accurately reflects the formulaic nature of the books themselves. It was only when Tor turned to the scintillating talent of Doug Beekman that the series began to boast something visually distinctive and exciting. His cover for **CONAN AND THE GRIM GREY GOD** by Sean Moore (1964-1998) is a thing of real beauty.

Probably the most interesting feature of the Tor series was the decision to release some, but by no means all, of the books first in trade paperback format before following them

*Continued overleaf*

# King of the Nemedian Chroniclers

The earliest Tor editions carried the following strange endorsement: "Nobody alive knows CONAN better than L. Sprague de Camp ...and L. Sprague de Camp says: "Nobody alive writes CONAN better than Robert Jordan."

It is difficult to judge from this exactly whose ego was being flattered most. But whatever purpose it sought to serve the statement was wholly erroneous on both counts. For if anyone deserved those accolades then, and merit them still, that person is Roy Thomas.

Between 1970 and 1980, and again from 1991 to 2000, Thomas wrote literally hundreds of Conan stories for Marvel Comics. He wrote them for comic books, black and white magazines, annuals, mini-series, treasury editions and graphic novels. He even wrote two years worth of a Conan newspaper strip. And much of what he wrote continues to eclipse even the most accomplished of the prose pastiches. It is probably fair to say that no one has done more to promote and popularise Howard's hero to greater effect, or more wide spread acclaim, than Thomas.

The groundbreaking early issues of the original **Conan the Barbarian** comic book, produced with artist Barry Windsor-Smith, were first collected in a series of six paperbacks published by Grosset and Dunlap between 1978 and 1979. And they have been repackaged umpteen times since. Thomas has recently recounted his work on the comic in his book *Barbarian Life: A literary Biography of Conan the Barbarian*.

It remains a source of ongoing regret to many Conan fans that Thomas was never afforded the opportunity to publish a Conan novel of his own. He did actually attempt one in the late 1970s but it was vetoed by De Camp on the patronising grounds that it was "too comicbooky". This seems somewhat ironic cause for complaint considering the cartoon Conan de Camp himself had both promulgated and presided over.

Thomas modestly maintains that he "probably wouldn't have [proven to be] Crom's answer to the earthly reincarnation of Robert E. Howard" but still laments the lost opportunity to find out either way. One can only hope that someone at Perilous Worlds might take note and extend an invitation to him to belatedly rectify a glaring omission in Conan publishing history.

*Richard Toogood*

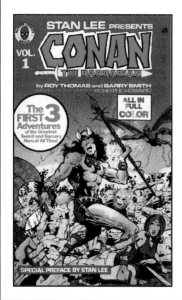

roughly a year after with mass market editions. There does not appear to be any particular rhyme or reason to explain why certain titles were singled out for this treatment and not others. Nor why both versions were packaged with completely different cover art.

The death of Lyon Sprague de Camp in the year 2000 marked a watershed in Conan publishing. Nearly all the Conan paperbacks that have appeared since then have comprised reissues of Howard's original stories. Only now those stories have been restored to their original states and shorn of all of De Camp's textual alterations and interpolations. The consequence of this is that almost any edition can now be recommended to any inquisitive

newcomer to Conan. The set of trade editions published by Ballantine/Del Rey between 2003 and 2005 remain the best from a purist perspective, having benefitted from all the scholarly diligence that went into the original Wandering Star/Book Palace Books hardback editions which are their source. But the three volumes issued by Gollancz in 2011 remain a convenient way of getting hold of Howard's original Conan canon. As does the cheap, but extremely cheerful, one volume trade version released by Prion in 2009.

With it now being more than eighty years since the death of Robert E Howard it seems inevitable that we will soon witness a proliferation of new Conan collections in both hard copy and e-book form, with enterprising publishers taking advantage of the fact that all the work Howard saw published in his own lifetime is now in the process of lapsing out of copyright. It may well soon prove all but impossible to compile an overview of this sort with any sort of pretensions towards comprehensiveness.

Since De Camp's death the only original non Howard Conan fiction to be published has been Harry Turtledove's widely derided 'Young Conan' novel *Conan of Venarium* released by Tor in 2003, and Michael Stackpole's novelisation of the 2011 Jason Momoa film.

The bulk of the Conan publishing edifice that has been built up over the course of the last fifty years now lies buried by the sands of out-of-print obscurity, rather like one of the haunted ruins of Howard's stories. But the news that Perilous Worlds will be restarting construction, beginning with a reissue of John C. Hocking's well regarded Tor effort *Conan and the Emerald Lotus*, may give rise to the hope that the best of the Conan pastiches published over the last five decades might also be disinterred at some point in the future.

Conan and the Emerald Lotus: *By general consensus John Hocking's 1995 novel is considered the best of the Tor series. A sequel entitled* Conan and the Living Plague *is forthcoming from Perilous Worlds.*

Printed in Great Britain
by Amazon